GLOBALIZATION

Buying and selling
the world

About the author
Wayne Ellwood established the North American office of New Internationalist and worked as a co-editor of the magazine until 2010. He has also worked as an associate producer with the groundbreaking BBC television series *Global Report* and edited the reference book *The A-Z of World Development*. He is also the author of *The NoNonsense Guide to Degrowth and Sustainability* (2013). He has travelled widely in Asia, Africa and Latin America. He lives in Toronto, Canada, where he is an editorial consultant and writer.

About the New Internationalist
New Internationalist is an award-winning, independent media co-operative. Our aim is to inform, inspire and empower people to build a fairer, more sustainable planet.

We publish a global justice magazine and a range of books, both distributed worldwide. We have a vibrant online presence and run ethical online shops for our customers and other organizations.

– **Independent media:** we're free to tell it like it is – our only obligation is to our readers and the subjects we cover.

– **Fresh perspectives:** our in-depth reporting and analysis provide keen insights, alternative perspectives and positive solutions for today's critical global justice issues.

– **Global grassroots voices:** we actively seek out and work with grassroots writers, bloggers and activists across the globe, enabling unreported (and under-reported) stories to be heard.

NONONSENSE

GLOBALIZATION
Buying and selling the world

Wayne Ellwood

NewInternationalist

BTL

NONONSENSE

Globalization
Buying and selling the world

Published in Canada by
New Internationalist Publications   and   Between the Lines
2446 Bank Street, Suite 653   401 Richmond Street West, Studio 281
Ottawa, Ontario   Toronto, Ontario
K1V 1A8   M5V 3A8
newint.org   btlbooks.com

First published in the UK in 2015 by New Internationalist Publications Ltd,
The Old Music Hall, 106-108 Cowley Road, Oxford OX4 1JE, UK

Series editor: Chris Brazier
Cover design by asmithcompany.co.uk
Series design by Juha Sorsa

Printed in Canada

Library and Archives Canada Cataloguing in Publication
Ellwood, Wayne
[No-nonsense guide to globalization]
Globalization : buying and selling the world / Wayne Ellwood. – Fourth edition.
(Nononsense)
Revision of: The no-nonsense guide to globalization / Wayne Ellwood. –
New updated ed. – Ottawa : New Internationalist Publications, ©2010.
Includes bibliographical references and index.
Issued in print and electronic formats. Co-published by: New Internationalist.
ISBN 978-1-77113-245-9 (paperback).–ISBN 978-1-77113-246-6 (epub).–
ISBN 978-1-77113-247-3 (pdf)
1. International economic relations. 2. Globalization. I. Title. II. Title: No-nonsense
guide to globalization. III. Series: NoNonsense (Toronto, Ont.)

HF1359.E46 2015   337   C2015-902392-0   C2015-902393-9

Between the Lines gratefully acknowledges assistance for its publishing activities from the
Canada Council for the Arts, the Ontario Arts Council, the Government of Ontario through
the Ontario Book Publishers Tax Credit program and through the Ontario Book Initiative, and
the Government of Canada through the Canada Book Fund.

Contents

Foreword

This is a wide-lensed and well-documented analysis of 'globalization' that lives up to its title. The years since its first publication in 2001 have confirmed and strengthened the original rich evidence of a totalizing depredation of the lives of the majority of the world's people and their life-support systems.

What readers find in this fully updated mini-classic is a rich spectrum of documented facts showing trends of degeneration of societies and life conditions that media and states fail to recognize and respond to. While their stories and policies remain as systemically disconnected from collective human needs as 15 years ago, this work provides a valuable record of the life-blind system's march through the world.

Beginning with Cristóbal Colón's search for new riches turning to genocides, through the US-dominated Bretton Woods and IMF financial framework to the borderless corporate takeover of the world economy as a global casino, and beyond that to the life-and-death issues of poverty and the environment that the ruling economic paradigm blinkers out, the basic facts are held intact through the pressures of an era without a collective memory of its past. The last 35 years of the great depredation of human and natural life systems on Earth have brought no significant policies to prevent the runaway transnational money machine driving the devastation. Even the overdue adaptations recommended in the final chapter remain closed out of international policy discussion.

An accessibly impartial study like this is essential for a minimally informed understanding of these degenerate trends. We cannot sustain humanity or life on Earth by a ceaseless repetition of slogans of 'growth', 'market reforms', and 'we must compete harder' as solutions to collapsing lives and life conditions of the rising majority of the world. The equivalent of a price of a cup coffee in increase of per-capita income is not being 'lifted out of poverty'. The master ideal of a 'self-regulating global free market' is absurd when tens of thousands of new corporate trade rules backed by financial embargo and armed force covertly institute the private demands of global money monoliths – with elected legislatures made subordinate.

Governments now compete to enact the prescribed agenda, or they disappear. Deregulated global capital floods elsewhere in nanoseconds. Dissenting politicians, parties and policies are ignored or pilloried in the press. This second-order reality of 'buying and selling the world' remains unspeakable to name, but this book reports basic life consequences tracked over a generation which are generally the opposite of 'a rising tide lifting all boats' and 'new freedom and prosperity for people across the world'.

Paradigm shift can only be achieved by re-grounding in the collective life capital of societies and ecosystems. Yet both continue to be stripped and despoiled by a runaway, private, money-sequence system multiplying itself as the final goal of humanity and the Earth. This system now spans all borders. *Globalization: Buying and Selling the World* tracks how the most powerful empire in history yields ever more riches to the richest – while hollowing out human and natural life systems.

John McMurtry FRSC,
Professor Emeritus
University of Guelph,
Ontario, Canada.

Introduction

When the first edition of this book was published 15 years ago, I described globalization as 'the most talked-about and perhaps the least understood concept of the new millennium'.

Much has changed in the intervening years. Globalization was a new buzzword back then. Today, libraries groan with thousands of books on the subject and a simple internet search will produce millions of 'hits'. Everyone has their own idea of what globalization means, even though the more closely we examine the concept the more ephemeral it gets.

Here's one thing we do know: the world we live in feels smaller. There is no doubt the digital age has brought us all closer together. Yet the new wired world is also more dangerous and divided. The fallout is nowhere more evident than in the devastating collapse of the global economy that began in 2008 and whose repercussions are still with us. It is paradoxical that, as national and regional economies become more intertwined, the idea of a global community with shared goals and values appears to be fading.

Before the economic crisis came the murderous attacks in New York and Washington on September 11, 2001 – a day that changed the course of world history and underlined the increasing contradictions of a globalized world. In response to those events, the US and its allies launched a protracted 'war on terror' which flouted both domestic and international law. This conflict has ebbed and flowed over the intervening years. But it has not abated. Attacks by deluded jihadists and freelance terrorists in France, Britain, Denmark and other Western countries have inflated the fear factor, paving the way for anti-terror legislation that both threatens civil liberties and erodes democratic freedoms. As a consequence, attempts to address the root causes of violence – poverty, political exclusion, alienation, anomie and growing inequality – have been largely shelved.

Since 2008 the wars in Iraq, Afghanistan, Pakistan, and more recently in Syria, plus the simmering conflict in Israel/Palestine, have been fought against a backdrop of global economic collapse. Despite thousands of dead, millions of refugees and billions of dollars wasted on weaponry, the situation in the Middle East remains unresolved. After more than a decade of fighting in Afghanistan, warlords still rule most of the country. The isolated regime in Kabul is hobbled by corruption and survives only with the help of Western arms and aid money. In Iraq and Syria the extremist Sunni group, Islamic State, is determined to carve an independent Islamist *caliphate* out of those war-ravaged nations.

We are now living through the most serious economic crisis since the Great Depression of the 1930s. The link to globalization, specifically to the worldwide deregulation of the finance and banking sectors, is visible to all. (The history of this shift to a 'global casino' built on lax government regulation of these industries is outlined in Chapter 5.) Facing catastrophe, governments stepped into the breach with billions in taxpayer funds to bail out the banks and keep the credit system solvent. They also ploughed billions into classic Keynesian stimulus packages to fend off economic collapse. Even once-powerful symbols of the industrial era like General Motors (GM) queued up for government handouts (GM received $50 billion from Washington in return for part-ownership of the company). AIG, the largest insurance company in the US, swallowed more than $180 billion in public funds. In total, the amounts the UK and the US earmarked to support their banks reached nearly 75 per cent of their combined GDP.

The cost in jobs, hunger, poverty and fear has been incalculable – a social catastrophe whose profound repercussions will echo through future decades.

Despite the economic and human carnage, bankers appear to have learned little. They have furiously opposed more stringent regulations at every step. And governments, for the most part, have been reluctant to introduce tough new laws, or even to enforce existing ones. America's first black President, Barack Obama, rode to victory on the promise of renewal, hope and sweeping change. Unfortunately, rhetoric has outstripped action. Executives at US financial firms shamelessly scooped up more than $26 billion in bonuses in 2013. And the 2010 Dodd-Frank law aimed at capping banker bonuses has quietly disappeared. The EU has been more aggressive, restricting bonuses to no more than twice fixed salaries. But even there bankers tried to dodge the new rules by adding 'allowances' not included in their yearly pay.

The perpetrators of the recent recession remain unbowed. Nonetheless, the economic crisis has opened deep cracks in the façade of global capitalism. It has become clear that the global economy is seriously out of joint. There is a growing outcry to reshape globalization into a force for improving the lives of the majority of the world's people.

Across Latin America the electorate has embraced democracy and rejected a free-trade model which has sacked national economies, subverted local cultures and thrown millions into poverty and unemployment. In Greece and Spain, protesters reacted with outrage and violence to government moves to slash public spending in the face of a credit crunch brought on by the global economic crisis. In January 2015, public outrage over staggering unemployment and widespread poverty as a result of EU-enforced cuts in Greece led to victory by the anti-austerity Syriza party. And in Spain mass protests by *los indignados* (the indignant ones) led to the rise of *Podemos* ('Yes, we can'), an anti-austerity party of the Left with ballooning public support.

At the international level there has been encouraging progress in building institutions that strengthen global citizenship and buttress international law – however imperfect. The UN Landmine Ban Convention, the International Tribunals on Former Yugoslavia and Rwanda and the International Criminal Court are three such initiatives. Less impressively, the UN Framework Convention on Climate Change continues to grope towards a serious program to combat global warming.

The reality of globalization may have seeped into the public consciousness over the last decade but the concept is as old as capitalism itself – a continuing saga of expanding trade and melding cultures. The world has been shrinking for centuries. Peppers, maize and potatoes, once found only in Latin America, are now common foods in India, Africa and Europe. Nutmeg, pepper and cloves, originally from Indonesia, thrive in the Caribbean. The descendants of black Africans, first brought as slaves to work the land of the 'new world', have become Americans, Jamaicans, Canadians, Brazilians and Guyanese.

But the 'old story' of globalization today has developed a new twist driven by technological change. The micro-electronics revolution of the past 30 years has irrevocably altered the essence of human communication. Digital technology has created a world of instant communications, creating what some have called the 'third wave' of economic growth.

The computer revolution that catalyzed the new global economy has been used in other, sometimes contradictory, ways. Images of conflict and violence can spread with lightning speed. And all sides have access to this new technology in the war of ideas. Opponents of globalization use email and cellphones to share photos, videos and text, to strategize across borders and to organize demonstrations. Meanwhile, Islamic State militants broadcast stark videos of terrified hostages threatened with beheading. So the images multiply and clash: the horrific torture of prisoners by US troops in Abu Ghraib; the inflammatory cartoons in *Charlie Hebdo* that ignited an explosion of violence; the global demonstrations against climate change; the outpouring of support for Black victims of police violence in Ferguson, Missouri. All are in some way the fruits of globalization.

Just as technology can stoke the fires of dissent and amplify events which once might have remained unknown, so the speed of global travel has turned the whole world into ground zero for lethal new diseases. The SARS epidemic in 2003 reached 31 countries in less than a month, while in 2014 the deadly Ebola virus again emerged in West Africa, spreading panic and raising fears of a global pandemic. The World Health Organization predicts that the avian flu virus, if it crosses to humans, could kill up to seven million people worldwide. The globalization of trade and the industrialization of animal husbandry are intimately linked to the spread of these new diseases.

This global exchange of people, products, plants, animals, technologies and ideas will continue for the foreseeable future – even as transport costs increase. For now at least the process is unstoppable.

Despite all the dangers, this new, more intimate world holds much promise. If we jointly recognize the common thread of humanity that binds us, how can globalization not be a positive force for change?

The Western tradition is steeped in optimism and the notion of progress. The basic credo is simple: economic growth is the measure of human development and a globally unified market is the ultimate goal. The expansion of international trade will lead to a more equal, more peaceful, less parochial world. Eventually, so the argument goes, global integration and cross-cultural understanding will create a borderless world where political differences are put aside in a new pact of universal humanity.

This is a compelling vision: we live in a deeply unequal world but it is one of enormous wealth and great opportunity. Despite the recent recession, there are more people living longer, healthier, more productive lives than at any time in human history. And much of that advance is due to the extraordinary capacity of modern capitalism to produce the goods.

But this success has been compromised by a corporate-led plan for economic integration which threatens human rights, cultural distinctiveness, economic independence and political sovereignty. Instead of helping to build a better world for all, the fundamentalist free-market model is eroding both democracy and equity. The social goals, the cohesive values that make us work as communities, are being ignored in the headlong rush for growth and profit.

The global economy teeters on the brink, gaps between rich and poor are widening, decision-making power is concentrated in fewer and fewer hands, local cultures are homogenized, biological diversity is destroyed, regional tensions are increasing and the environment is nearing the point of collapse. That is the face of globalization today, an opportunity for prosperity whose potential has been hijacked.

This small book attempts to sketch an admittedly incomplete picture of that global economic system – its history, its structure, its failings – and the forces in whose interest it works.

By understanding how we got here and what is at stake, we can perhaps find a route out of the current economic crisis and in the process redefine globalization. The solutions are still embryonic. But the debate is lively. The events of the past few years only reinforce the conclusion that radical change is long overdue.

Wayne Ellwood
Toronto, 2015

1 Globalization then and now

Globalization is a relatively new word which describes an old process: the integration of the global economy that began in earnest with the launch of the European colonial era five centuries ago. But the process has accelerated over the past 30 years with the explosion of computer technology, the dismantling of barriers to the movement of goods and capital, and the expanding political and economic power of transnational corporations.

More than five centuries ago, in a world without electricity, cellphones, antibiotics, refrigeration, wifi, automobiles, jet aircraft or nuclear weapons, one man had a foolish dream. Or so it seemed at the time. Cristóbal Colón, an ambitious young Genoese sailor and adventurer, was obsessed with Asia – a region about which he knew nothing, apart from unsubstantiated rumors of its colossal wealth. Such was the strength of his obsession (some say his greed) that he was able to convince the King and Queen of Spain to bankroll a voyage into the unknown across a dark, seemingly limitless expanse of water then known as the Ocean Sea. His goal: to find the Grand Khan of China and the gold that was rumored to be there in profusion.

Centuries later, Colón would become familiar to millions of schoolchildren as Christopher Columbus, the famous 'discoverer' of the Americas. In fact, the 'discovery' was more of an accident. The intrepid Columbus never did reach Asia – not even close. Instead, after five weeks at sea, he found himself sailing under a tropical sun into the turquoise waters of the Caribbean, making his landfall somewhere in the Bahamas, which he promptly named San Salvador (the Savior). The place clearly delighted Columbus' weary crew. They loaded up with fresh water and unusual foodstuffs. And they were befriended by the island's indigenous population, the Taíno.

'They are the best people in the world and above all the gentlest,' Columbus wrote in his journal. 'They very willingly showed my people where the water was, and they themselves carried the full barrels to the boat, and took great delight in pleasing us. They became so much our friends that it was a marvel.'[1]

Twenty years and several voyages later, most of the Taíno were dead and the other indigenous peoples of the Caribbean were either enslaved or under attack. Globalization, even then, had moved quickly from an innocent process of cross-cultural exchange to a nasty scramble for wealth and power. As local populations died off from European diseases or were literally worked to death by their captors, thousands of European colonizers followed. Their desperate quest was for gold and silver. But the conversion of heathen souls to the Christian faith gave an added fillip to their plunder. Eventually European settlers colonized most of the new lands to the north and south of the Caribbean.

Columbus' adventure in the Americas was notable for many things, not least his focus on extracting as much wealth as possible from the land and the people. But, more importantly, his voyages opened the door to 450 years of European colonialism. And it was this centuries-long imperial era that laid the groundwork for today's global economy.

Colonial roots

Although globalization is now a commonplace term, many people would be hard-pressed to define what it actually means. The lens of history provides a useful beginning. Globalization is an age-old process and one firmly rooted in the experience of colonialism. One of Britain's most famous imperial spokespeople, Cecil Rhodes, put the case for colonialism succinctly and brazenly in the 1890s. 'We must find new lands,' he said, 'from which we can easily obtain raw materials and at the same time exploit the cheap slave labor that is available from the natives of the colonies. The colonies [will] also provide a dumping ground for the surplus goods produced in our factories.'[2]

During the colonial era European nations spread their rule across the globe. The British, French, Dutch, Spanish, Portuguese, Belgians, Germans, and later the Americans, took possession of most of what was later called the Third World. And of course they also expanded into Australia, New Zealand/Aotearoa and North America. In some places (the Americas, Australia, New Zealand and southern Africa) they did so with the intent of establishing new lands for European settlement. Elsewhere (Africa and Asia) their interest was more in the spirit of Rhodes' vision: markets and plunder. From 1600 to 1800 incalculable riches were siphoned out of Latin America to become the chief source of finance for Europe's industrial revolution.

Global trade expanded rapidly during this period as colonial powers sucked in raw materials from their new dominions: furs, timber and fish from Canada; slaves and gold from Africa; sugar, rum and fruits from the Caribbean; coffee, sugar, meat, gold and silver from Latin America; opium, tea and spices from Asia. Ships crisscrossed the oceans. Heading towards the colonies, their holds were filled with settlers, administrators and manufactured goods; returning home, the stout galleons and streamlined clippers bulged with coffee, copra, cotton and cocoa. By the 1860s and the 1870s world trade was booming. It was a 'golden era' of international commerce – though the European powers pretty much stacked things in their favor. Wealth from their overseas colonies flooded into France, England, Holland and Spain while some of it also flowed back to the colonies as investment – in railways, roads, ports, dams and cities. Such was the range of global commerce in the 19th century that capital transfers from North to South were actually greater at the end of the 1890s than at the end of the 1990s. By 1913 exports (one of the hallmarks of increasing economic integration) accounted for a larger share of global production than they did in 1999.

Expanding international trade

When people talk about globalization today they're still talking mostly about economics, about an expanding international trade in goods and services based on the concept of 'comparative advantage'. This theory was first developed in 1817 by the British economist David Ricardo in his *Principles of Political Economy and Taxation*. Ricardo wrote that nations should specialize in producing goods in which they have a natural advantage and thereby find their market niche. He believed this would benefit both buyer and seller but only if certain conditions were maintained, such as: 1) trade between partners must be balanced so that one country doesn't become indebted and dependent on another; and 2) investment capital must be anchored locally and not allowed to flow from a high-wage country to a low-wage country.

Unfortunately, in today's high-tech world of instant communications, neither of these key conditions exists. Ricardo's blend of local self-reliance mixed with balanced exports is nowhere to be seen. Instead, export-led trade dominates the global economic agenda. The only route to increased prosperity, say the 'experts', is to expand exports to the rest of the world. The rationale is that all countries and all peoples eventually benefit from more trade.

When the world economic crisis erupted in 2008, international trade slumped for the first time in living memory. According to the World Trade Organization (WTO), trade in Europe fell by nearly 16 per cent in the fourth quarter of 2008 while global trade fell by more than 30 per cent in the first quarter of 2009. But this was an anomaly. During the 1990s world trade grew by an average 6.6 per cent yearly and from 2000

Tyranny and poverty

Colonialism in the Americas separated Indians from their land, destroyed traditional economies and left native people among the poorest of the poor.

- The Spanish ran the Bolivian silver mines with a slave labor system known as the *mita*; nearly eight million Indians had died in the Potosí mines by 1650.
- Suicide and alcoholism are common responses to social dislocation. Suicide rates on Canadian Indian reserves are 10 to 20 times higher than the national average.
- In Guatemala the infant mortality rate among indigenous people is 30% higher than for the non-indigenous population. Maternal mortality is almost 10 times higher among indigenous people. (cesr.org)

Indian Population of the Americas: 1492 and 1992

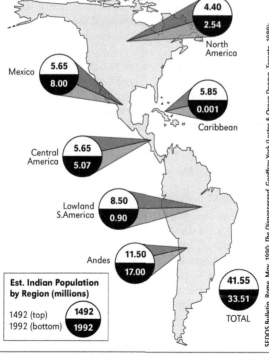

North America
4.40 / 2.54

Mexico
5.65 / 8.00

Caribbean
5.85 / 0.001

Central America
5.65 / 5.07

Lowland S.America
8.50 / 0.90

Andes
11.50 / 17.00

TOTAL
41.55 / 33.51

Est. Indian Population by Region (millions)

1492 (top)
1992 (bottom)

SEDOS Bulletin, Rome, May, 1990; *The Dispossessed*, Geoffrey York (Lester & Orpen Dennys, Toronto, 1989); *Guatemala: False Hope, False Freedom*, James Painter (CIIR, London, 1987); Ecuador Urgent Action Bulletin (Survival International, London, 1990); *Native Population of the Americas in 1492*, Ed. W. Denevan (University of Wisconsin Press, 1976) and GAIA Atlas of First Peoples, Julian Burger (Doubleday, New York, 1990).

on it averaged more than 6-per-cent growth a year. On average, trade after 1950 expanded twice as fast as world GDP. Unfortunately, most of this wealth ended up in the hands of the rich developed nations. They account for the lion's share of world trade and they mostly trade with each other. According to the WTO, in 2013 Europe and North America together accounted for nearly 50 per cent of global merchandise exports and 61 per cent of commercial service exports.[3]

Nonetheless, the world has changed in the last century in ways that have completely altered the character of the global economy and its impact on people and the natural world. Today's globalization is vastly different from both the colonial era and the immediate post-World War Two period. Even arch-capitalists like currency speculator George Soros have voiced doubts about the values that underlie the direction of the modern global economy.

'Insofar as there is a dominant belief in our society today,' he writes, 'it is a belief in the magic of the marketplace. The doctrine of *laissez-faire* capitalism holds that the common good is best served by the uninhibited pursuit of self-interest... Unsure of what they stand for, people increasingly rely on money as the criterion of value... The cult of success has replaced a belief in principles. Society has lost its anchor.'

The inefficient magic of the marketplace

The 'magic of the marketplace' is not a new concept. It's been around in one form or another since the father of modern economics, Adam Smith, published his pioneering work *The Wealth of Nations* in 1776. (Coincidentally, in that same year, Britain's 13 restless American colonies declared independence from the motherland.) But Smith's concept of the market was a far cry from the one championed by today's globalization boosters. Smith was adamant that markets worked most efficiently when there was equality between buyer and seller, and when neither was large enough to influence the market price. This, he said, would ensure that all parties received a fair return and that society as a whole would benefit through optimal use of its natural and human resources. Smith also believed that capital was best invested locally so that owners could see what was happening with their investment and could have hands-on management of its use. Author and activist David Korten sums up Smith's thinking as follows: 'His vision of an efficient market was one composed of small owner-managed enterprises located in the communities where the owners resided. Such owners would share in the community's values and have a personal stake in its future.'[4] Smith's understanding of the market bears little similarity to today's globalized economy, dominated by faceless mega-corporations with marginal ties to the local community. Corporate managers make decisions aimed at increasing shareholder value while ownership is vested in mysterious holding companies and distant financial conglomerates.

As Korten hints, our world is vastly different from the one that Adam Smith inhabited. Take the revolution in communications technology which only began around 1980. In less than four decades, mind-boggling advances in digital technology, software and satellite communications have radically altered the production, marketing, sales, and distribution of goods and services as well as patterns of global investment. Coupled with improvements in air freight and ocean transport, companies can now move their offices and factories to wherever costs are lowest. Being close to the target market still counts but it is no longer vital. Improved technology and relatively inexpensive oil (for the moment, anyway) have led to a massive increase in goods being transported by air and sea. The United Nations' International Civil Aviation Organization (ICAO) notes that global air traffic has doubled in size every 15 years since 1977. The agency predicts that it will double again by 2030. 'The 3.1

billion airline passengers carried in 2013 are expected to grow to about 6 billion by 2030, and the number of departures is forecast to grow from 32 million in 2013 to some 60 million in 2030.'[5] Airbus, the giant European aircraft manufacturer, predicts that air-freight traffic will continue to grow by five per cent yearly, mainly in so-called 'emerging' economies. Increased 'South-to-South' trade flows, Airbus says, will make up 16 per cent of global air freight by 2033.[6]

The global shipping business, which now consumes more than 140 million tons of oil a year, is expected to rebound dramatically once the global economy gets back on track. And costs are falling.

According to the Washington-based World Shipping Council, approximately 1,500 shipping companies make 26,000 US port calls a year while more than 50,000 container loads of imports and exports from 175 countries

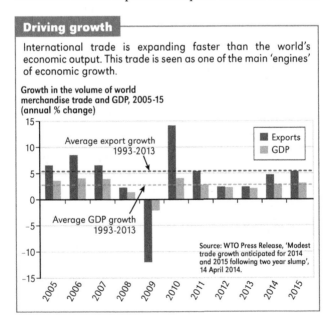

Driving growth

International trade is expanding faster than the world's economic output. This trade is seen as one of the main 'engines' of economic growth.

Growth in the volume of world merchandise trade and GDP, 2005-15 (annual % change)

Average export growth 1993-2013

Average GDP growth 1993-2013

Exports
GDP

Source: WTO Press Release, 'Modest trade growth anticipated for 2014 and 2015 following two year slump', 14 April 2014.

Globalization

are handled each day. From 1990 to 2005, rates on the three major US trade shipping routes fell by between 23 and 46 per cent.

It is not hyperbole to suggest that containerized shipping both changed the shape of industrial production and spurred globalization. When the container was introduced in 1956, the world was full of small manufacturers selling locally, much like Smith's ideal. A half century later local markets had mostly evaporated as plunging shipping costs opened up the global market. Combined with cheap labor, it meant the cost of long-distance shipping was no longer an issue. A garment factory in Bangladesh could fill an order for 10,000 shirts from Target, Sears or Marks and Spencer for a fraction of the cost of a local manufacturer. You could call it the 'footloose' phase of capitalism. Companies could bounce from country to country in search of cheap labor, low taxes and investment 'incentives' from job-hungry national governments.

Ocean-freight unit costs have fallen by 70 per cent since the 1980s, while air-freight costs have fallen by three to four per cent a year on average in recent decades.

These cheap transport rates reflect 'internal' costs – packaging, marketing, labor, debt and profit. But they don't reflect the 'external' impact on the environment of the irreplaceable fossil fuels used to power jet airliners and ocean freighters. Moving more goods around the planet increases pollution, contributes to ground-level ozone (ie smog) and boosts greenhouse-gas emissions, a major source of global warming and climate change. These ecological costs are basically ignored in the profit-and-loss equation of business. This is one of the main reasons environmentalists object to the globalization of trade. Companies make the profits but society has to foot the bill.

Enter the free-market fundamentalists

The other key to recent globalization springs from

Third World

If there's a Third World, then there must be a First and Second World too. When the term was first coined in 1952 by the French demographer, Alfred Sauvy, there was a clear distinction, though the differences have become blurred over the past few decades. Derived from the French phrase, tiers monde, the term was first used to suggest parallels between the tiers monde (the world of the poor countries) and the tiers état (the third estate or common people of the French revolutionary era). The First World was the North American/European 'Western bloc' while the Soviet-led 'Eastern bloc' was the Second World. These two groups had most of the economic and military power and faced off in a tense ideological confrontation commonly called the 'Cold War'. Third World countries in Africa, Latin America, Asia and the Pacific had just broken free of colonial rule and were attempting to make their own way rather than become entangled in the tug-of-war between East and West. Since the break-up of the Soviet Union in the early 1990s the term Third World has less meaning and its use is diminishing. Now many refer to the 'developing nations', the Majority World or just the South.

structural changes to the world economy that have occurred since the late 1970s. It was then that the system of rules set up at the end of World War Two to manage global trade collapsed. The fixed currency-exchange regime agreed at Bretton Woods, New Hampshire, in 1944 gave the world 35 years of relatively steady economic growth.

But around 1980 things began to shift with the emergence of fundamentalist free-market governments in Britain and the US, and the disintegration of the state-run command economy in the Soviet Union. The formula for economic progress adopted by the administrations of Margaret Thatcher in the UK and Ronald Reagan in the US called for a drastic reduction in the regulatory role of the state. According to their intellectual influences, Austrian economist, Friedrich Hayek, and University of Chicago academic, Milton Friedman, meddlesome big government was the problem. Instead, government was to take its direction from the market. Companies must be free to move their operations anywhere in the world to minimize costs and maximize returns to investors. Free trade, unfettered investment, deregulation, balanced budgets, low inflation and privatization of publicly owned enterprises were trumpeted as the six-step plan to national prosperity.

The deregulation of world financial markets went hand in hand with an emphasis on free trade. Banks, insurance companies and investment dealers, whose operations had been mostly confined within national borders, were suddenly unleashed. In London, deregulation took place on 24 October 1986 and was quickly dubbed the 'Big Bang'. Within a few years, major players from Europe, Japan and North America expanded into each other's markets as well as into the newly opened and fragile financial-services markets in the Global South. Aided by sophisticated computer systems (which made it easy to transfer huge amounts of money at the click of a mouse) and governments desperate for investment, the big banks and investment houses were quick to invest surplus cash anywhere they could turn a profit. In this new relaxed atmosphere, finance capital became a profoundly destabilizing influence on the global economy.

Instead of long-term investment in the production of real goods and services, speculators in the global casino make money *from* money – with little concern for the impact of their investments on local communities or national economies. Governments everywhere now fear the destabilizing impact of this 'hot money' which can come and go at the drop of a hat. The collapse of 2008 – the most devastating since the Great Depression of the 1930s – is just the latest in a long chain of financial disasters. Recent UN studies show a direct correlation between the frequency of financial crises and the huge increase in international capital flows from 1990 to 2010.

The East Asian financial crisis

The collapse of the East Asian currencies, which began in July 1997, was a catastrophic example of the damage caused by nervous short-term investors. Until then the 'tiger economies' of Thailand, Taiwan, Singapore, Malaysia and South Korea had been the success stories of globalization. Advocates of open markets pointed to these countries as proof that classic capitalism would bring wealth and prosperity to millions in the developing world – though they conveniently ignored the fact that in all these countries the State took a strong and active role in the economy. According to dissident ex-World Bank Chief Economist Joseph Stiglitz: 'The combination of high savings rates, government investment in education and state-directed industrial policy all served to make the region an economic powerhouse. Growth rates were phenomenal for decades and the standard of living rose enormously for tens of millions of people.'[7]

Foreign investment was tightly controlled in the 'tiger economies' until the early 1990s, severely in South Korea and Taiwan, less so in Thailand and Malaysia. Then, as a result of continued pressure from the International Monetary Fund (IMF) and others, the 'tigers' began to open up their capital accounts and private-sector businesses began to borrow heavily.

Spectacular growth rates floated on a sea of foreign investment as offshore investors poured dollars into the region, eager to harvest double-digit returns. In 1996, capital was flowing into East Asia at almost $100 billion a year. But mostly the cash went into risky real-estate ventures or into the local stock market where it inflated share prices far beyond the value of their underlying assets.

In Thailand, where the Asian 'miracle' first began to sour, over-investment in real estate left the market glutted with $20 billion worth of unsold properties. The house of cards collapsed when foreign investors began to realize that Thai financial institutions to which they had lent billions could not meet loan repayments. Spooked by the specter of falling profits and a stagnant real-estate market, investors called in their loans and cashed in their investments – first slowly, then in a panic-stricken rush.

More than $105 billion left the region in the next 12 months, equivalent to 11 per cent of the domestic output of the most seriously affected countries – Indonesia, the Philippines, South Korea, Thailand and Malaysia.[8] Having abandoned capital controls, Asian governments were powerless to stop the massive hemorrhage of funds. Ironically, the IMF's 1997 *Annual Report*, written just before the crisis, singled out Thailand's 'remarkable economic performance' and 'consistent record of sound macroeconomic policies'.

The IMF was to be proven wrong – disastrously so. Across the region economic output plummeted while unemployment soared, leaping by a factor of 10 in Indonesia alone. The human costs of the East Asian economic crisis were immediate and devastating. As bankruptcies soared, firms shut their doors and millions of workers were laid off. More than 400 Malaysian companies declared bankruptcy between July 1997 and March 1998 while in Indonesia – the poorest country affected by the crisis – 20 per cent of the population, nearly 40 million people, were pushed into poverty. The impact of the economic slowdown had the devastating effect of reducing both family income and government expenditures on social and health services for years afterwards. In Thailand, more than 100,000 children were yanked from school when parents could no longer afford tuition fees. The crash also had a knock-on effect outside Asia. Shock-waves surged through Latin America, nearly tipping Brazil into recession while the Russian economy suffered worse damage. Growth rates slipped into reverse and the Russian ruble became nearly worthless as a medium of international exchange.

The East Asian crisis was a serious blow to the

'promise' of globalization – and a stiff challenge to the orthodox economic prescriptions of the IMF. Indeed, in retrospect, the Asian meltdown of 1997-98 can be seen as a warm-up for the debacle of 2007-09. Across the region, the Fund was reviled as the source of the economic disaster. The citizens of East Asia saw their interests ignored in favor of Western banks and investors. In the end, writes Stiglitz: 'It was the IMF policies which undermined the market as well as the long-run stability of the economy and society.'

It was the first time that the 'global managers' and

Pinball capital

Short-term speculative capital whizzes around the world leaving ravaged economies and human devastation in its wake. East Asia (Indonesia, South Korea, Thailand, Malaysia, the Philippines) suffered a destructive net reversal of private capital flows from 1996 to 1997 of $12 billion.

Percentage change in GDP before and after the Asian financial crisis

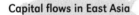

	Thailand	Indonesia	Malaysia	S.Korea
Average 1980-90	7.6	6.1	5.2	9.4
Average 1990-96	8.3	7.7	8.7	7.3
Average 1997	–7	–16	–6	–6

Capital flows in East Asia

INFLOW $93 billion 1996

OUTFLOW $105 billion 1997

finance kingpins showed that the system wasn't all it was made out to be. The world economy was more fragile, and thus more explosive, than anybody had imagined. As the region slowly recovered, citizens around the world began to scratch their heads and wonder about the pros and cons of globalization, especially the wisdom of unregulated investment. The mass public protests against the WTO, the IMF/World Bank and the G8 were still to come – in Seattle, Prague, Genoa, Quebec City, Doha and elsewhere. But the East Asian crisis planted worrying seeds of doubt about the merits of corporate globalization.

1 Kirkpatrick Sale, *The Conquest of Paradise: Christopher Columbus and the Columban Legacy*, Knopf, New York, 1990. **2** *The Ecologist*, Vol 29, No 3, May/June 1999. **3** 'Modest trade growth anticipated for 2014 and 2015 following two year slump', WTO press release, 14 April 2014. **4** David Korten, *When Corporations Rule the World*, Kumarian/Berrett-Koehler, West Hartford/San Francisco, 1995. **5** *The World of Air Transport in 2013*, Annual Report of the ICAO Council. **6** *Global Market Forecast 2014 Freight*, Airbus S.A.S. **7** Joseph Stiglitz, *Globalization and its Discontents*, WW Norton, New York/London, 2003. **8** *Human Development Report 1999,* United Nations Development Programme, New York/Oxford, 1999.

2 The Bretton Woods trio

The Great Depression of the 1930s leads to the birth of Keynesianism and the interventionist state. As World War Two ends, the victors put together a new set of rules for the global economy. This post-War financial architecture includes the World Bank, the International Monetary Fund (IMF) and the General Agreement on Tariffs and Trade (GATT). But, as Third World nations emerge from centuries of colonialism, these institutions are seen increasingly as pillars of the status quo.

As World War Two was drawing to a close, the world's leading politicians and government officials, mostly from the victorious 'Allied' nations (mainly Britain, the United States, the Soviet Union, Canada, France, Australia and New Zealand) began to think about the need to establish a system of rules to run the post-War global economy.

Before the outbreak of the War in 1939, trading nations everywhere had been racked by a crippling economic depression. When the US stock market crashed in October 1929 the shockwaves were felt around the world. Nations turned inward in an attempt to pull themselves out of a steep economic skid. But without a system of global rules there was no coherence or larger logic to the 'beggar-thy-neighbor' polices adopted worldwide. High tariff barriers were hastily erected between countries with the result that world trade nosedived, economic growth spluttered and mass unemployment and poverty followed. From 1929 to 1932 global trade fell by an astounding 62 per cent while global industrial production slumped by 36 per cent. As a result the 1930s became a decade of radical politics and rancorous social ferment in the West as criticism of *laissez-faire* ('let it be') capitalism and an unchecked market economy grew.

Scholars like Hungarian exile Karl Polanyi helped reinforce a growing suspicion of a market-based economic model which put money and investors at the center of its concerns rather than social values and human wellbeing. 'To allow the market mechanism to be the sole director of the fate of human beings and their natural environment... would result in the demolition of society,' Polanyi wrote in his masterwork, *The Great Transformation*.

Polanyi was not alone in his distrust of the market economy. Other thinkers, like the brilliant British economist John Maynard Keynes, were also grappling with a way of controlling global markets, making them work for people and not the other way around. Keynes both admired and feared the power of the market system. With the example of the Great Depression of the 1930s fresh in his mind he predicted that, without firm boundaries and controls, capitalism would be immobilized by its own greed, and would eventually self-destruct. As it happened, only World War Two turned things around. The War set the factories humming again as millions of troops were deployed by all sides in the conflict. Arms manufacturers, aircraft factories and other military suppliers ran 24-hour shifts, primed by government spending. Then, as the War wound down, government policymakers began to think about how to ensure a smooth transformation to a peacetime economy.

Keynesian economics

It was Keynes' radical notion of an 'interventionist' state to which governments turned in an effort to rebuild their economies. Until the worldwide crash of the 1930s, the accepted economic wisdom had been that a degree of unemployment was a 'normal condition' of the free market. The economy might go up or down according to the business cycle but in the long run, growth (and increased global trade), would create new jobs and sop up the unemployed.

Keynes was skeptical about this *laissez-faire* orthodoxy. He believed that the economy was a human-made artifact and that people acting together through their government could have some control over its direction. We must act now, he suggested, since 'in the long run we're all dead'. With no other solutions in the wings, his approach offered a lifeline for governments who found themselves helplessly mired in economic stagnation.

In *The General Theory of Employment, Interest and Money* published in 1936, Keynes argued that the free market, left on its own, actually creates unemployment. Profitability, he pointed out, depends on suppressing wages and cutting costs by replacing labor with technology. In other words, profits and a certain amount of unemployment go hand in hand – so far so good, at least for those making the profits. But Keynes went on to show that lowering wages and sacking workers would eventually backfire. There would be fewer people who could afford to buy the goods that factories were producing. As demand fell, so would sales; factory owners would be forced to lay off even more workers. This, reasoned Keynes, was the start of a downward spiral with terrible human consequences.

To 'prime the pump', he suggested that governments should intervene actively in the economy. He reasoned that business owners and rich investors are unlikely to open their wallets if the prospects for profit look dim. When the economy is floundering, argued Keynes, that's when governments should step in – by spending on public goods (education, healthcare, job training) and on 'infrastructure' (roads, sewers, dams, public transport, electricity), and by giving direct financial support to the jobless.

Even if governments had to go into debt to kick-start growth Keynes advised politicians not to worry. The price was worth it. By directly stimulating the economy, government could rekindle demand and help reverse the downward spiral. Once their confidence returned, companies would begin to invest again to increase production to meet the growing demand. This would mean hiring more workers who would soon have more money in their pockets. As jobs increased, so would taxes, from workers and from businesses. Eventually, the government would be able to pay back its debt with increased tax revenues from a now healthy, growing economy.

Desperate Western governments were quick to adopt Keynes' answer to economic stagnation. In the US, the 'New Deal' policies of the Roosevelt administration were directly influenced by Keynes. The American Employment Act of 1946 accepted the federal government's responsibility 'to promote maximum employment, production and purchasing power'. The British government, too, in 1944 accepted as one of its primary aims 'the maintenance of a high and stable level of employment after the war'.

Other countries like Canada, Australia and Sweden quickly followed. Keynes' influence spread and people began to believe that economics was more than a 'dismal science', the term coined by the 19th-century British historian Thomas Carlyle. Maybe it could actually be managed to make the world a more prosperous and predictable place.

'We are witnessing a development under which the economic system ceases to lay down the law to society and the primacy of society over that system is secured.' Thus wrote Karl Polanyi, in a moment of supreme optimism just before the end of the war.

It was this confidence that delegates from 44 nations brought to the postcard-pretty resort village of Bretton Woods, New Hampshire, in July 1944. The aim of the UN Monetary and Financial Conference was to erect a new framework for the post-War global economy – a stable, co-operative international monetary system which would promote national sovereignty and prevent future financial crises. The purpose was not to bury capitalism but to save it. The main proposal was for a system of fixed exchange rates. In the light of the Depression of the previous decade, floating rates were now seen as inherently unstable and destructive of national development plans.

Keynes' influence at Bretton Woods was huge. But despite his lobbying and cajoling he did not win the day on every issue. The US opposed his 'soft' approach and in the end the enormous military and economic clout of the Americans proved impossible to overcome.

The Conference rejected his proposals to establish a world 'reserve currency' administered by a global central bank. Keynes believed this would have created a more stable and fairer world economy by automatically recycling trade surpluses to finance trade deficits. Both deficit *and* surplus nations would take responsibility for trade imbalances. However, his solution did not fit the interests of the US, eager to take on the role of the world's economic powerhouse in the wake of World War Two. Instead the Conference opted for a system based on the free movement of goods with the US dollar as the international currency. The dollar was linked to gold and the price of gold was fixed at $35 an ounce (28 grams). In effect the US dollar became 'as good as gold' and in this one act became the dominant currency of international exchange – a position which it still holds, despite growing pressure from China and others to come up with an alternative.

Three governing institutions emerged from the gathering to oversee and co-ordinate the global economy. These were not neutral economic mechanisms: they contained a powerful bias in favor of the industrialized nations, global competition and corporate enterprise. And each had a distinct role to play.

1 The International Monetary Fund (IMF)

The IMF was born with a mission: to create economic stability for a world which had just been through the trauma of depression and the devastation of war. As originally conceived, it was supposed to 'facilitate the expansion and balanced growth of international trade' and 'to contribute to the promotion and maintenance of high levels of employment and real income'.

A major part of its job was to oversee a system of 'fixed' exchange rates. The aim was to stop countries from devaluing their national currencies to win a competitive edge over their neighbors – a defining feature of the economic chaos of the 1930s.

The Fund was also to promote currency 'convertibility' to encourage world trade – to make it easier to exchange one currency for another when trading across national borders.

And finally the new agency was to act as a 'lender of last resort' supplying emergency loans to countries that ran into short-term cashflow problems.

Keynes took a different tack. He wanted to set up an International Clearing Union which would automatically provide unconditional loans to countries experiencing balance-of-payments problems. These loans would be issued 'no strings attached' with the purpose of supporting domestic demand and maintaining employment. Otherwise countries feeling the pinch would be forced to balance their deficit by cutting imports, lowering wages and dampening domestic demand in favor of exports.

Keynes stressed that international trade was a two-way street and that the 'winners' (those countries in surplus) were as obligated as the 'losers' (those countries in deficit) to bring the system back to balance. Keynes suggested that pressure be brought to bear on surplus nations so they would be forced to increase their imports and recycle the surplus to deficit nations.

But Keynes did not prevail. Instead a proposal put forward by US Treasury Secretary Harry Dexter White became the basis for the IMF. The International Clearing Union idea disappeared. IMF members would not automatically receive loans when they fell into deficit.

Instead members would have access to limited loan amounts which were to be determined by a complex quota system. Voting power within the IMF would be based on the level of financial contributions – one dollar, one vote – which meant that rich countries would call the shots.

When a country joins the IMF it is assigned a quota which is calculated in Special Drawing Rights (SDRs), the Fund's own unit of account. Quotas are assigned according to a country's relative position in the world economy, which means that the most powerful economies have the most influence. In 2014, for example, the US had the largest SDR quota at 42.1 billion (about $65 billion) while the smallest member, the Pacific island nation of Tuvalu, had an SDR quota of 1.8 million (about $2.78 million). The size of a member's quota determines a lot, including how many votes it has in IMF deliberations and how much foreign exchange it has access to if it runs into choppy financial waters.

Nonetheless, the IMF was founded on the belief that collective action was necessary to stabilize the world economy, just as nations needed to unite together at the UN to bring stability to the global political system.

The final decision was that balance-of-payments loans are contracted at less than the prevailing interest rate and members are supposed to use and repay them within five years. The issue of whether the IMF could attach conditions to these loans was unclear in the original Bretton Woods agreement. But Harry Dexter White was crystal clear six months later when he wrote in the journal *Foreign Affairs* that the Fund would not simply dole out money to debtor countries. The IMF would force countries to take measures which, under the old gold standard, would have happened automatically.

The delegates at the Bretton Woods Conference supported a gradual reduction of trade barriers and tariffs. The consensus was that the state should focus on jobs, growth and the wellbeing of its citizens –

intervening in the market if necessary. But they were less keen on allowing the free movement of capital, which was seen to undercut the policy of fixed exchange rates.

Keynes advocated a balanced world trade system with strict controls on the movement of capital across borders. He held that the free movement of goods *and* capital, advocated most powerfully by the US delegation, would inevitably lead to inequalities and instabilities. This battle he won at Bretton Woods: capital controls remained in place, more or less, for the next 35 years.

2 The World Bank

One of the other key goals of the Bretton Woods Conference was to find a way to rebuild the economies of those nations that had been devastated by World War Two. The International Bank for Reconstruction and Development was created to spearhead this effort. The Bank is funded by dues from its members and by money borrowed on international capital markets. It makes loans to members below rates available at commercial banks. Its initial mandate was to provide financing for 'infrastructure' which included things like power plants, dams, hospitals, roads, airports, ports, agricultural development and education systems. The Bank poured money into reconstruction in Europe after World War Two. But it was not enough to satisfy the US, whose booming industries were in need of markets. In response the US set up its own 'Marshall Plan', named after then Secretary of State, George Marshall. From April 1948 to December 1951 the US provided $12.5 billion to 16 European nations, largely in the form of grants rather than loans.

As Europe gradually recovered, the Bank turned from 'reconstruction' to 'development' in the newly independent countries of the Third World, where it became widely known as the World Bank. As Southern countries sought to enter the industrial age, the Bank became a major player throughout the region. According to the 'stages of growth' economic theory popular at the time, developing nations could achieve economic 'take-off' only from a strong infrastructure 'runway'. It was part of the Bank's self-defined role to build this 'infrastructural capacity' and this it did enthusiastically by funding dams, hydroelectric projects and highway systems throughout Latin America, Asia and Africa.

But despite the Bank's low lending rates it was clear early on that the very poorest countries would have difficulty meeting loan repayments. So in the late 1950s the Bank was pressured into setting up the International Development Association. This wing of the Bank was to provide 'soft loans' with very low interest or none at all. It was not all altruism – it was also designed to head off Third World countries from setting up an independent aid agency under UN auspices, separate from the Bretton Woods institutions. In addition, the Bank established two other departments: the International Finance Corporation, which supports private-sector investment in Bank-approved projects, and the Multilateral Insurance Guarantee Agency, which provides risk insurance to foreign corporations and individuals that decide to invest in one of the Bank's member countries.

3 General Agreement on Tariffs and Trade (GATT)/ World Trade Organization (WTO)

Although Bretton Woods delegates debated the idea of an International Trade Organization there was no consensus. The Americans balked at the idea that trade should be linked to employment policy or that poor countries should get a fairer price for their commodity exports. So the General Agreement on Tariffs and Trade (GATT) emerged in 1947 to set rules on global trade in industrial goods only. Its aim was to reduce the national trade barriers and to stop the beggar-thy-neighbor policies that had so hobbled the global economy prior to World War Two. After seven rounds of tariff negotiations over the next 40 years GATT members reduced tariffs from 40-50 per cent to 4-5 per cent.

The final 'Uruguay Round' began in 1986. In March 1994, following its completion, politicians and bureaucrats met in Marrakech, Morocco, to approve a new World Trade Organization (WTO) to replace the more loosely structured GATT. The WTO is officially an international organization rather than a treaty. And unlike the Bank and the Fund it does not set rules. Instead it provides a forum for negotiations and then ensures that agreements are followed. By June 2014 there were 160 member states, accounting for over 98 per cent of world trade. There were also 25 'observers' including eight countries negotiating to join the WTO: Afghanistan, Bhutan, Comoros, Equatorial Guinea, Ethiopia, Liberia, São Tomé & Príncipe and Sudan.

The WTO vastly expands GATT's mandate. The text of the WTO agreement had 26,000 pages: a hint of both its prolixity and its complexity. It includes the GATT agreements which mostly focus on trade in goods. But it also folds in the new General Agreement on Trade in Services (GATS), which potentially reduces barriers to investment in more than 160 areas – including basic needs like water, healthcare and education as well as telecommunications, banking and investment, transport and the environment. GATS is not a treaty. It's more like a framework agreement where negotiations can continue indefinitely. For large global corporations it's a potential goldmine of new business opportunities.

From the outset GATT was seen as a 'rich man's club' dominated by Western industrial nations slow to concede their position of power. The WTO continues this tradition of rich-world domination. Rubens Ricupero, former Secretary-General of the UN Conference on Trade and Development (UNCTAD), is frank in his assessment of the multilateral trading system. It is a matter of 'concrete evidence', he said at the September 1999 G77 (developing countries 'Group of 77') Ministerial

Meeting in Morocco, that global trade rules are 'highly imbalanced and biased against developing countries'. Why is it, asked Ricupero, that developed countries have been given decades to 'adjust' their economies to imports of agricultural products and textiles from the South when poor countries are pressured to open their borders immediately to Western banks and telecommunication companies? As a case in point he mentions the Multi Fibre Arrangement (MFA) on textiles under which industrial countries were allowed to impose quotas restricting clothing and textile imports from developing nations. The MFA developed from a waiver which the US demanded on behalf of its domestic cotton industry in the late 1950s. By the time the MFA was phased out in January 2005 it had lasted nearly 50 years – a ridiculously long time for a 'temporary' concession which was

The gold standard

Until the Great Depression of the 1930s gold was the one precious metal that most large trading countries in the world recognized and accepted as a universal medium of exchange. The shift to gold began when international trade exploded after the industrial revolution. Britain was the first to adopt the gold standard in 1816; the US made the change in 1873 and by 1900 most of the world had joined them.

Most national currencies were redeemable in gold. Paper bank notes often contained the phrase 'the bank promises to pay the bearer on demand' the equivalent in gold. That implied you could go into a bank and demand the equivalent in gold if the mood moved you.

What that meant was that all nations set the value of their national currency in terms of ounces of gold (1 ounce = 28g). It was a convenient way of settling national trading accounts. And the fixed gold standard was supposed to both stabilize foreign exchange rates and domestic economies. A country's wealth could be measured by the amount of gold it had stored in its vaults; certainly an unfair advantage for those countries lucky enough to be sitting on vast natural deposits of gold.

With gold as a fixed standard the fluctuations of international trade were relatively simple to track. If a country's imports exceeded its exports then gold had to be shipped to those countries who were owed in order to balance the books. The decline in the to allow US producers to adjust to cheap textile imports.[1]

In contrast, according to the UN Development Programme (UNDP), developing countries have been much more willing to open their borders to foreign imports and reduce trade barriers. The average tariff in developing countries fell from 25 per cent in the late 1980s to 11 per cent by the end of 2004. India, for example, reduced its tariffs from an average of 82 per cent in 1990 to 7.2 per cent by the end of 2013. Brazil chopped average tariffs from 25 per cent to 7.9 per cent over the same period and China lowered them from 43 per cent in 1993 to 4.1 per cent in 2013. According to UNDP, only 79 per cent of exports from the least developed countries were given duty-free access to the markets of developed countries in 2007. In addition, OECD[2] (developed) countries continued to subsidize

---

amount of gold would then force a government to reduce the amount of cash in circulation. Because money was redeemable for gold both governments and banks would want to make sure they could cover themselves if necessary. Less money in circulation would tend to lower prices, dampening economic activity at home and decreasing imports. Gold flowing to countries on the receiving end would have the opposite effect. Governments would release more cash into the economy to cover the increase of gold in their vaults and prices would tend to increase.

With the Depression of the 1930s one country after another abandoned the gold standard in an attempt to 'devalue' their currencies to gain a 'competitive advantage' over their trading partners (ie to make their exports cheaper). There was an attempt to modify the gold link after World War Two when the US set the value of the dollar at 1/35 of an ounce (0.9g) of gold but holders of cash were no longer able to demand gold in exchange and the circulation of gold coins was prohibited. Then in 1973 US President Richard Nixon suspended the exchange of American gold for foreign-held dollars at fixed rates. At that point gold became just another commodity, its price determined by the law of supply and demand. Many countries (as well as the International Monetary Fund) continue to hold vast gold reserves and quantities are occasionally sold on the open market – though sellers are careful not to flood the market and depress the international price too much.

agriculture to the tune of $258.6 billion in 2012 – a little more than twice the $125.6 billion total of official foreign aid that year. In North America the US spent over $30 billion and Canada more than $7.5 billion on agricultural subsidies in 2012.

Notes UNDP: 'The world's highest trade barriers are erected against some of its poorest countries. On average, trade barriers faced by developing countries exporting to rich countries are three to four times higher than those faced by rich countries when they trade with each other.'[3]

How the WTO has its way

The WTO pursues its free-trade agenda with the single-minded concentration of the true believer. Nonetheless, there is a growing unease about the organization's globalizing agenda. Critics are especially wary of the Dispute Resolution Body (DRB), which gives the WTO the legal tools to approve tough trade sanctions by one member against another, especially against nations that might disagree with the organization's interpretation of global trade rules. Any member country, acting on behalf of a business with an axe to grind, can challenge the laws and regulations of another country on the grounds that they violate WTO rules.

Previously, if GATT wanted to discipline one of its members for not playing according to the rules, every member had to agree. The WTO has considerably more power. The DRB appoints a panel of 'experts' who hear the case behind closed doors. If the panel decides on sanctions the only way to escape them is if every WTO member is opposed to adopting them – a virtual impossibility. In effect, the WTO regime is one of trade *über alles*. Environmental laws, labor standards, human rights legislation, public health policies, cultural protection, food self-reliance or any other policies held to be in the 'national interest' can be attacked as unfair 'impediments' to free trade.

Already there have been cases where the WTO has effectively struck down national legislation in its pursuit of a 'level playing field'. The 1999 WTO decision against the European Union (EU) over importing bananas is a case in point. The WTO's 'most favored nation' clause demands that similar products from different member countries be treated equally. Under the terms of the Lomé Convention (a trade and aid agreement between the EC and 71 African, Caribbean, and Pacific countries first signed in February 1975 in Lomé, Togo) the EU had promised to give preference to bananas from former European colonies in Africa, the Caribbean and the Pacific. In general these banana growers tend to be small farmers, typically with plots of less than four hectares, who are less dependent on pesticide-intensive plantation methods than the giant US companies like Dole and Chiquita. Bananas account for between 20 and 60 per cent of export earnings in the Caribbean.

The Europeans stressed their right to determine a sovereign foreign policy in relation to former colonies while the US argued that EU tariffs prohibited American banana companies in Latin America from reaching lucrative markets in Europe. The WTO decided on behalf of the US, ruling that the European preference was unfair. Meanwhile, small island nations in the Caribbean, so dependent on income from the banana trade, worried that the decision would wipe out their major market in Britain and destroy their industry. By 2005 their fears seemed to be coming true. The number of registered banana growers in the Windward Islands (Dominica, Grenada, St Lucia and St Vincent and the Grenadines) had fallen from about 24,000 in 1993 to fewer than 5,000 in 2005. Meanwhile, banana-industry earnings tumbled from 20 per cent of the islands' GDP in the early 1990s to less than five per cent of GDP in 2005.[4]

Quotas on the import of 'third country' (ie Latin American) bananas into the EU were finally eliminated in January 2006. (The Lomé Convention was replaced in

June 2000 by the Cotonou Agreement, named after the town in Benin where the deal was signed.)

All nations have the right to use the Dispute Resolution Body to pursue their economic self-interest. But the fact is that the world's major trading nations are also its most powerful economic actors. So the tendency is for the strong to use the new rules to dominate weaker countries. The 'national treatment clause' basically says that a country may not discriminate against products of foreign origin on any grounds whatsoever. And in so doing it removes the power of governments to develop economic policy which serves the moral, ethical or economic interests of their citizenry. WTO rules prohibit members from barring products if they disagree with the 'Processes and Methods of Production'. For example, if t-shirts or shoes are produced by children in sweatshop conditions, that is not considered germane. The same is true if a foreign factory fouls the air, if poverty wages are paid to workers or if the goods themselves are poisonous and dangerous.

According to WTO rules, any country that refuses to import a product on the grounds that it may harm public health or damage the environment has to prove the case 'scientifically'. So Canada, the world's biggest asbestos producer, petitioned the WTO's dispute panel and won – forcing the EU to lift its ban on the import of the known carcinogen. And when the EU refused imports of hormone-fed beef from North America, the US took the case to the WTO arguing that there was no threat to human health from cows fed on hormones. The EU ban on hormone-fed beef also applied to the region's own farmers but that made little difference. The WTO's dispute resolution panel decided in favor of the US, effectively ruling that Europeans had no right to pass laws that supported their opposition to hormones. The EU was ordered to compensate producers in the US and Canada for every year of lost export earnings. And in retaliation the WTO allowed the US to impose

$116 million worth of sanctions on a range of European imports – including Dijon mustard, pork, truffles and Roquefort cheese.

Meanwhile, in 2001 the giant US-based shipping company, United Parcel Service (UPS), lodged a complaint with the North American Free Trade Agreement (NAFTA) – which runs a dispute resolution body similar to the WTO – threatening Canada's government-run postal service. UPS charged that Ottawa is unfairly subsidizing Canada Post and therefore poaching potential customers. In response, the Council of Canadians and the Canadian Union of Postal Workers (CUPW) asked Ontario's Superior Court of Justice to rule NAFTA's investment rules as unconstitutional.

'UPS claims that simply by having a public postal system, Canada is allowing unfair competition,' charged Council Chair Maude Barlow. 'By this logic, every public service from healthcare to education could face similar lawsuits. We don't intend to let foreign corporations destroy our public services.'

In June 2007, the UPS claim was denied when the NAFTA tribunal hearing the challenge dismissed the $160-million suit against the Canadian government.

A year earlier, the WTO sided with Canada, the US and Argentina in a dispute with the EU over genetically engineered crops. The WTO argued that the EU discriminated against biotech seeds without adequate scientific evidence. US agribusiness claimed the ban cost American firms $300 million a year in sales to the EU. Critics, however, called the WTO decision a 'direct attack on democracy' – undaunted, EU governments voted in 2005 to reaffirm their ban on GM seeds.[5]

And so it goes in the topsy-turvy world of economic globalization. Those institutions which first emerged from the Bretton Woods negotiations half a century ago have become more important players with each passing decade. It is their vision and their agenda which continue to shape the direction of the global economy.

Together, they are fostering a model of liberalized trade and investment which is heartily endorsed by the world's biggest banks and corporations. A deregulated, privatized, corporate-led free market is the answer to humanity's problems, they tell us. The proof, though, is not so easily found.

1 Martin Khor, 'WTO must correct imbalances against South', *Third World Network Features*, Oct 1999. **2** OECD stands for Organization for Economic Co-operation and Development – 34 of the most developed countries are members. **3** *Human Development Report 2005*, UNDP, New York, 2005. **4** 'Caribbean Bananas: The Macroeconomic Impact of Trade Preference Erosion', *IMF Working Paper*, M Mlachila, P Cashin, C Haines, March 2010. **5** 'Biotech industry gets boost', *Toronto Star*, 8 Feb 2006.

3 Debt and structural adjustment

Developing countries fight for a New International Economic Order, including fairer terms of trade, and push their case through UN agencies like UNCTAD and producer cartels like OPEC. Petrodollars flood Northern financial centers and US President Richard Nixon floats the dollar, sabotaging the Bretton Woods fixed exchange-rate system. When Third World debt expands, the IMF and World Bank step in to bail out debt-strapped nations. In return they must adopt 'structural adjustment' policies which favor cheap exports and spread poverty throughout the South.

The global economy has changed dramatically since 1980 – so much so that few of us today recall the campaign for a 'new international economic order' (NIEO) by African, Asian and Latin American nations just 10 years before that. Throughout the 1960s and early 1970s, an insistent demand for radical change burst forth from the two-thirds of the world's people who lived outside the privileged circle of North America and western Europe. There was a strong movement to shake off the legacy of colonialism and to shape a new global system based on economic justice between nations. Some Third World states began to explore ways of increasing their bargaining power with the industrialized countries in Europe and North America by taking control of their natural resources. The Organization of Petroleum Exporting Countries (OPEC) was formed in September 1960 by four Middle East oil producers (Iran, Iraq, Kuwait, Saudi Arabia) plus Venezuela. Their goal was to control the supply of petroleum and ratchet up the price of oil, thereby increasing their share of global wealth and bringing prosperity to their populations. The oil exporters' success led to heady talk of 'producer cartels' to raise the price of other exports like tin, nickel, coffee, cocoa, cotton and natural rubber so that poor countries dependent on one or two primary commodities could gain more income and control over their own development. There was also strong opposition to the growing power of Western-based corporations that were seen to be remaking the world in their own interests, trampling on the rights of weaker nations. When poor countries tried to increase the price of their main exports, they often found themselves confronting the near-monopoly control by big corporations of processing, distribution and marketing.

In the wake of OPEC, the NIEO was strongly endorsed at the Summit of Non-Aligned Nations in Algiers in September 1973. Then, in April 1974, the Sixth Special Session of the UN adopted the *Declaration and Program of Action of the New International Economic Order*. The following December the General Assembly approved the *Charter of Economic Rights and Duties of States*.

Key NIEO demands included:

- 'Indexing' developing-country export prices to tie them to the rising prices of manufactured goods from the developed nations.
- Hiking official aid from the developed countries to 0.7 per cent of GNP (only Sweden, Norway, Luxembourg, Denmark and the Netherlands have consistently reached or exceeded this 0.7% target in the succeeding years).
- Lowering tariffs on exports from poor countries and managing volatile commodity markets.
- Regulating transnational corporations to ensure they comply with national laws.
- Greater stability in exchange rates and monitoring of cross-border capital flows.

Meanwhile, the *Charter of Economic Rights and Duties of States* endorsed:

- The sovereignty of each country over its natural resources and economic activities, including the right to nationalize foreign property.

- The right of countries dependent on a small range of primary exports to form producer cartels.

The declaration of NIEO principles was the culmination of a new 'solidarity of the oppressed' which had spread throughout the developing nations.

The 'Third World' seeks justice

Galvanized by centuries-old colonial injustices and sparked by the radical ideas of Frantz Fanon in Algeria, Kwame Nkrumah in Ghana, Mohandas Gandhi in India, Sukarno in Indonesia, Julius Nyerere in Tanzania and Fidel Castro in Cuba, these 'Third World' nations set out to collectively challenge the entrenched power of the United States and western Europe. The NIEO was not a grassroots movement. It was a collection of intellectuals and politicians who believed that free markets, left to themselves, would never reduce global inequalities – there needed to be a global redistribution of wealth. For the most part they did not reject the capitalist model. Instead these leaders argued for improved 'terms of trade' and a more just international economic system. When bargaining failed, producer countries began to form trade alliances based on specific commodities.

Third World nations also formed political organizations like the Non-Aligned Movement, which was initially an attempt to break out of the polarized East/West power struggle between the West and the Soviet Bloc. In the UN, developing countries formed the 'Group of 77', which was instrumental in creating the UN Conference on Trade and Development (UNCTAD). Within UNCTAD, poor countries pushed for fairer 'terms of trade'. Many newly independent countries in the South still relied heavily on the export of raw materials in the 1950s and 1960s. But there was a faltering effort and a stronger belief in the need to build local industrial capacities and to push for a new global economy based on justice and fairness. Why was it that the price of imports from the West – whether manufactured goods, spare parts or foodstuffs – seemed to creep ever upwards while the prices for agricultural exports and raw materials from the South remained the same – or even decreased? This patent injustice was one of the main concerns of the NIEO and the focus of its commodity program.

The plan was to intervene in the market, to regulate supplies and steady prices, to the benefit of both producers *and* consumers. The 10 core commodities were to be cocoa, coffee, tea, sugar, jute, cotton, rubber, 'hard' fibers (sisal and coir), copper and tin. This new commodity system was to be based on 'international buffer stocks' with a 'common fund' to purchase these stocks when prices dropped, as well as new multilateral trade commitments and improved 'compensatory financing' to stabilize export earnings. Unfortunately, the NIEO was never really given much of a chance by Western nations, which saw it as an erosion of their market advantage. They rejected out of hand the idea that rich countries had anything to do with the plight of developing countries. They denied that poor countries had shared interests and they refused to accept that these countries were sidelined by international institutions. Third World nations, meanwhile, were split by divergent interests, a desperate need for export earnings and their lack of political power.

The transparent injustice of this enraged and frustrated leaders like Tanzania's charismatic Julius Nyerere, who referred to declining terms of trade as constantly 'riding the downward escalator'. Between 1980 and 1991 alone, non-oil exporting developing countries lost nearly $290 billion due to decreasing prices for their commodity exports. In response to this economic discrimination, developing countries also began agitating for an increase in 'untied' aid from the West. (When aid was 'tied', poor countries were obliged to spend their aid dollars on goods and services from the donor nation; it was in fact a way of subsidizing domestic manufacturers.) Third World nations also called for more liberal terms on development loans and for a quicker transfer of new manufacturing technologies from North to South.

In addition, most developing countries favored an active government role in running the national economy. They quite rightly feared that in a world of vast economic inequality they could easily be crushed between self-interested Western governments and their muscular corporate partners. This was the chief reason that many Third World nations began to take tentative steps to regulate foreign investment and to introduce minimal trade restrictions.

This process began in Latin America, where formal political independence had been won in the 19th century, much earlier than in Asia and Africa. South American nations began to encourage 'import substitution' in the 1950s as a way of boosting local manufacturing, employment and income. Countries like Brazil and Argentina used a mix of taxation policy, tariffs and financial incentives to attract both foreign and domestic investment. US and European auto companies set up factories to take advantage of import barriers. The goal was to stimulate industrialization in order to produce goods locally and to boost export earnings. This had the added benefit of reducing imports, which both cut the need for scarce foreign exchange and kept domestic capital circulating inside the country. But the era of import substitution was short. Latin American nations were bullied into dismantling import barriers. Foreign-made goods, mostly American, soon flooded in again, undercutting domestic industries. By the late 1980s, there were few local producers of cars, TVs, fridges or other major household goods in Latin America. Production that remained was dominated by big foreign companies. Nonetheless, the attempt at import substitution was an important step in trying to shift the balance of global power to poor countries.

The origins of the debt crisis

Even before the clamor for a new international economic order, momentous changes were beginning to unfold that would dramatically alter the fate of poor nations for decades to come. By the late 1960s, the Bretton Woods dream of a stable monetary system – fixed exchange rates with the dollar as the only international currency – was collapsing under the strain of US trade and budgetary deficits.

As the US war in Vietnam escalated, the Federal Reserve in Washington pumped out millions of dollars to finance the conflict. The US economy was firing on all cylinders and beginning to overheat dangerously. Inflation edged upwards while foreign debt ballooned to pay for the war.

World Bank President Robert McNamara also leapt into the fray and contracted huge loans to the Global South during the 1970s – both for 'development' (defined as basic infrastructure to bring 'backward' economies into the market system) and to act as a bulwark against a perceived worldwide communist threat. The Bank's stake in the South increased five-fold over the decade.

At the same time, a guarded optimism took hold in developing countries, fuelled by moderately high growth rates and a short-term boom in the price of commodities, particularly oil. OPEC was the first, and ultimately the most successful, Third World 'producer union'. By controlling the supply of oil, it was able to triple the price of petroleum to over $30 a barrel. The result was windfall surpluses for OPEC members – $310 billion for the period 1972-77 alone. This 'oil shock' rippled through the global economy, triggering double-digit inflation and a massive currency 'recycling' problem.

What were OPEC nations to do with this vast new wealth of 'petrodollars'? Some of the cash was spent on glittering new airports, power stations and other showcase mega-projects. But much of it eventually wound up as investment in Northern financial centers or deposited in Northern commercial banks. This enormous inflow of petrodollars led to the birth of the 'eurocurrency' market – a huge pool of money held outside the borders of the countries that originally issued the currency. The US dollar was the main 'eurocurrency' but there were also francs, guilders, marks and pounds.

Western banks, with all this new OPEC money on deposit, began to search for borrowers. They didn't have to look for long. Soon millions in loans were contracted to non-oil-producing Third World governments desperate to pay escalating fuel bills and to fund ambitious development goals. At the same time the massive increase in oil prices triggered a surge in global inflation. Prices skyrocketed while growth slowed to a crawl and a new word was added to the lexicon of economists: 'stagflation'.

In the midst of this economic chaos, US President Richard Nixon moved unilaterally to delink the dollar from gold. A key goal of Bretton Woods was to 'ensure exchange-rate stability, prevent competitive devaluations, and promote economic growth'. The US dollar was to provide that stability by functioning as a global currency. (The US owned over half the world's official gold reserves – 574 million ounces – at the end of World War Two.) International trade was to be settled in dollars which could be converted to gold at a fixed exchange rate of $35 an ounce. The US government agreed to back every overseas dollar with gold. Other currencies were fixed to the dollar and the dollar was pegged to gold.

Nixon's radical move torpedoed Bretton Woods and moved the world to a system of floating exchange rates. Washington also devalued the US dollar against other major world currencies, jacked up interest rates to attract investment and imposed a 90-day wage-and-price freeze to fight inflation – all of which had an enormous impact on the global economy.

By slashing the value of the dollar, Washington

effectively reduced the huge debt it owed to the rest of the world. The US had been running a sizeable deficit to pay the costs of the war in Vietnam. As interest rates shot up, those countries reeling under the effect of OPEC oil-price hikes had the cost of their eurodollar loans (most of which were denominated in US dollars) double or even triple almost overnight. The debt of the non-oil-producing Third World increased five-fold between 1973 and 1982, reaching a staggering $612 billion. The banks were desperate to lend to meet their interest obligations on deposits, so easy terms were the order of the day. Dictators who could exact payments from their cowering populations with relative ease must have seemed like a good bet for lenders looking for a secure return.

Sometimes the petrodollar loan money was squandered on grandiose and ill-considered projects. Sometimes it was simply filched – siphoned off by Third World elites into personal accounts in the same Northern banks that had made the original loans. Often it was both wasted and stolen.

Dictator kickbacks and 'odious debt'

The experience was similar across the Global South. From the mid-1960s to the mid-1980s, despots were in power across Latin America and they employed an ingenious variety of scams. In Asia and Africa, too, autocrats with powerful friends and voracious appetites for personal wealth were financed willingly by the international banking fraternity. Indeed, it worked so well that the credit lines became almost limitless – particularly if the governments in question were on the 'right' side of the Cold War and buying large quantities of arms from Northern suppliers.

Examples of these foolish loans to corrupt leaders are well known. In the Philippines, the dictator Ferdinand Marcos with his wife, Imelda, and their cronies, pocketed in the form of kickbacks and commissions a third of all loans to that country. Before he was forced from office in 1986, Marcos' personal wealth was estimated at $10 billion.

The Argentine military dictatorship, famous for its 'dirty war' against so-called subversives, borrowed $40 billion from 1976 to 1983 and left no records for 80 per cent of the debt. After the return to democracy Argentineans demanded that the government either produce accounts or declare the debt illegal. Evidence soon emerged that some US banks knew money was being misused, that there had been kickbacks plus fraudulent loans to companies linked to the military, and that the IMF allegedly connived at the fraud. The military also used some of the money to buy weapons for the Falklands/Malvinas War. Later, in the 1990s, following the IMF prescription, President Carlos Menem privatized public services and industries and pegged the Argentine peso to the US dollar. All for naught as it turned out – in 2001 the crushing debt burden led to a complete collapse of the Argentinean economy. Bank accounts were frozen. The country defaulted on nearly half its $180-billion repayment obligations the following year and there was tremendous popular pressure to resist taking on further foreign debt.

Analyst Joseph Hanlon cites the African country of Zaire (now the Democratic Republic of the Congo) as another flagrant example of loans made knowingly to 'corrupt and nasty dictators'. In 1965, Joseph Mobutu, a staunch anti-communist, seized power in the Congo, which he renamed Zaire. The IMF country director, Irwin Blumenthal, also acted as head of Zaire's central bank from 1978. Hanlon quotes a memo from Blumenthal in which the IMF employee writes that corruption was so serious that there was 'no (repeat no) prospect for Zaire's creditors to get their money back'. Despite this warning, the IMF funnelled $700 million to Mobutu over the next decade while the World Bank pumped in another $2 billion. Western governments also shoved cash at the dictator. Hanlon notes: 'When Blumenthal wrote his report, Zaire's debt was $4.6 billion. When Mobuto was overthrown and died in 1998, the debt was $12.9 billion.'[1]

From 1997 to 2000, the 'Jubilee 2000' citizens' movement led a worldwide campaign to cancel the debts of the world's poorest countries. The campaign attracted millions of supporters, North and South. Jubilee researchers found that almost a quarter of all Third World debt (then around $500 billion) was the result of loans used to prop up dictators in some 25 different countries – sometimes called 'odious debt'. 'Odious', because citizens wondered why they should be obliged to repay loans contracted by corrupt rulers who used the money to line their own pockets.

Loans flowed free and fast through the 1970s and early 1980s. But eventually the soaring tower of debt began to crack and sway. One government after another began to run into trouble. The loans they had squandered on daft projects or salted away in private bank accounts became so large that foreign-exchange earnings and tax revenues couldn't keep up with the payments.

Structural adjustment

During this period, the IMF became an enforcer of tough conditions on poor countries that were forced to apply for temporary balance-of-payments assistance. The loans were conditional on governments following the advice of Fund economists who had their own take on what Southern nations were doing wrong and how they could fix it. The demands were woven into the deals worked out with those countries that required an immediate transfusion of cash. Essentially, the IMF argued that the debtor country's problems were caused by 'excessive demand' in the domestic economy. Curiously, the responsibility of the private banks that made most of the dubious loans in the first place (with their eyes wide open, it should be noted) was ignored.

According to the Fund, this excessive local demand meant there were too many imports and not enough exports. The proposed solution was to devalue the currency (making imports more expensive) and cut government spending. This was supposed to slow the economy and reduce domestic demand, gradually resulting in fewer imports, as well as more and cheaper exports. In time, the IMF argued, a little belt-tightening would eliminate the balance-of-payments deficit.

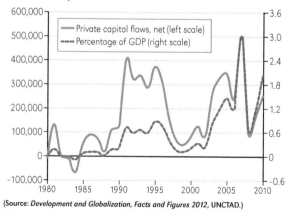

South pays North

Most of the increase in debt in recent years has been to pay interest on existing loans rather than for productive investment or to tackle poverty. Developing countries have often paid out more in debt service (interest plus principle) than they receive in loans and new investment – a net transfer from North to South. After the crash of 2008, net private capital flows to developing countries plummeted. Ironically this reversal could be beneficial in the long run since private capital is often speculative and destabilizing. As financial globalization has spread rapidly in recent decades more and more developing countries have liberalized their financial systems.

Net private capital flows towards developing and transition economies, 1980-2010 ($ millions and as percentage of recipient countries' GDP)

Private capital flows, net (left scale)
Percentage of GDP (right scale)

(Source: *Development and Globalization, Facts and Figures 2012*, UNCTAD.)

Countries were forced to adopt these austerity measures if they wanted to get the IMF 'seal of approval'. Without it, they would be ostracized to the fringes of the global economy. As early as the 1970s, both the IMF and the World Bank also urged debtor nations to take on deeper 'structural adjustment' measures. Initially, borrowing countries refused to go along with the advice.

Then, in 1982, Mexico became the first indebted country to admit it could no longer meet its payments and a fully fledged Third World 'debt crisis' emerged. Northern politicians and bankers began to worry that the huge volume of unpayable loans would undermine the world financial system. Widespread panic began to spread as scores of Southern nations teetered on the brink of economic collapse. In response, both the Bank and the IMF hardened their line and demanded major changes in the way debtor nations ran their economies. Countries like Ghana were forced to impose tough adjustment conditions as early as 1983. A few years later, US Treasury Secretary James Baker decided to formalize this new strategy, forcing Third World economies to radically 'restructure' their economies to meet their debt obligations. The 'Baker Plan' was introduced at the 1985 meeting of the World Bank and the IMF when the US urged both agencies to impose more thorough 'adjustments' on debtor nations.

The Bank and the Fund made full use of this new leverage. Together they launched a policy to 'structurally adjust' the Third World by further deflating economies. They demanded a withdrawal of government funding from public enterprise but also from basic healthcare, welfare and education. Exports to earn foreign exchange were privileged over basic necessities, food production and other goods for domestic use.

The IMF set up its first 'formal' Structural Adjustment Facility in 1986. The World Bank, cajoled by its more doctrinaire sibling, soon followed – by 1989 the Bank had contracted adjustment loans to 75 per cent of the countries that already had similar IMF loans in place. The Bank's conditions extended and reinforced the IMF prescription for financial 'liberalization' and open markets.

These new demands included:

- selling state-owned enterprises to the private sector;
- reducing the size and cost of government through public-sector layoffs;
- cutting basic social services as well as subsidies on essential foodstuffs;
- reducing barriers to trade.

This restructuring was highly lucrative for the financial sector. Private banks siphoned off more than $178 billion from the Global South between 1984 and 1990.[2] Structural-adjustment programs (SAPs) were an extremely effective mechanism for transforming private debt into public debt.

Consequently, the 1980s were a 'lost decade' for much of the Third World – especially for Africa. Growth stagnated and debt doubled to almost $1,500 billion by the decade's end. By 2002, it had reached nearly $2,500 billion. An ever-increasing proportion of this new debt was to service interest payments on the old debt, to keep money circulating and to keep the system running. Much of this debt had shifted from private banks to the IMF and the World Bank – though the majority was still owed to rich-world governments and Northern banks. The big difference was that the Fund and the Bank were always first in line, so paying them was a much more serious prospect.

The stark fact that the IMF and the Bank were taking more money out of the developing countries than they were putting in was a jolt for those who believed those institutions were there to help.

In six of the eight years from 1990 to 1997 developing countries paid out more in debt service (interest plus repayments) than they received in new loans: a total transfer from South to North of $77 billion. Most of the increase was to meet interest payments on existing debt

Creating poverty

In return for new loans to poor countries, lenders in the 1980s and 1990s insisted on 'structural adjustment' to increase their chances of being paid back. This meant cutting government spending on things like healthcare and education – the very services on which poor people (and women and children in particular) rely. Many of these countries have ended up spending more on servicing their debts than on the basic needs of their citizens.

Government spending on foreign debt and social services (selected countries, 2012)

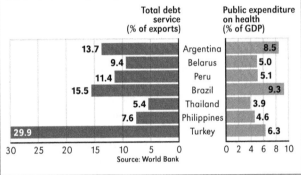

	Total debt service (% of exports)	Country	Public expenditure on health (% of GDP)
	13.7	Argentina	8.5
	9.4	Belarus	5.0
	11.4	Peru	5.1
	15.5	Brazil	9.3
	5.4	Thailand	3.9
	7.6	Philippines	4.6
	29.9	Turkey	6.3

Source: World Bank

rather than for new productive investment.[3] In 1998, this negative flow reversed as a result of massive bailout packages to Mexico and Asia. Nonetheless, figures for all private and public loans received by developing countries between 1998 and 2002 show that Southern nations repaid $217 billion more than they received in new loans over the same period.[4]

According to the Jubilee Debt Campaign (JDC) the total debt of the very poorest countries in 2007 (the 'low income countries' with an annual average income then of less than $935 per person) was $222 billion. That same year, those countries paid over $12.4 billion to the rich world in debt service – $34 million a day. For all 'developing' countries, total external debt in 2007 was $3,400 billion on which they paid $540 billion in debt service. There was some debt cancellation in 2008 and 2009, but there were also massive new debts in response to the global financial crisis.

Meanwhile, the 'conditions' imposed by structural adjustment diverted government revenues away from things like education and healthcare towards debt repayment and the promotion of exports. This gave the World Bank and IMF a degree of control over national sovereignty that the most despotic of colonial regimes rarely achieved.

Even former 'economic shock-therapy' enforcers like Columbia University's Jeffrey Sachs were forced to reconsider their faith in this 'neoliberal' recipe for economic progress. In 1999, Sachs wrote that many of the world's poorest people live in countries 'whose governments have long since gone bankrupt under the weight of past credits from foreign governments, banks and agencies such as the World Bank and the IMF... Their debts should be cancelled outright and the IMF sent home.'[5]

The limited scope of debt relief

Despite Sachs' warning, the situation has changed little. In nations as far apart as Rwanda, Egypt and Peru, the privations suffered in the name of debt repayments were hidden behind violent outbreaks of civil unrest. All attempts at debt relief for the South were rebuffed on principle until 1996, when the 'Heavily Indebted Poor Countries Initiative' (HIPC) was launched to make debt repayments 'sustainable'. This was followed in 2005 by the IMF-led Multilateral Debt Relief Initiative (MDRI) which offered full debt relief to those countries that fulfilled their HIPC obligations. The MDRI applies only to debts contracted with the IMF, the International Development Association (the World Bank's 'soft loan' window) and the African Development Fund. It doesn't offer relief on debts incurred to other governments, to private creditors or to other multilateral institutions.

According to the World Bank, by 2014 the HIPC and MDRI programs had relieved 36 countries of $96 billion in debt since 1996, 'freeing up their governments to spend money on poverty reduction'. Thirty-one of the beneficiary countries are in Africa.[6] But the HIPC/MDRI package has a checkered history. HIPC was designed in the interest of the creditors to protect their interests, to avoid default and to keep the system running. The program cancels debt to a level it considers 'sustainable' – based on a country's export earnings. But it doesn't consider other needs or whether the debts were legitimate in the first place. Poor countries are hobbled but not broken: they continue to spend billions on debt repayments, often as much as 20 per cent of revenues. And as the Jubilee Debt group suggests, much of that debt is 'unpayable' – it's simply impossible for countries to pay it off while also providing their people with health and education. Most HIPC candidates continue to spend more on debt service than on public health.[7] Despite $130 billion in debt cancellation from 2000 to 2013 the Jubilee Debt Campaign warns that the root causes of the debt trap are still in place and that 'history may be set to repeat itself'.

In October 2014 it noted: 'Two-thirds of impoverished countries face large increases in the share of government income spent on debt payments over the next 10 years. On average, current lending levels will lead to increases of between 85 per cent and 250 per cent in the share of income spent on debt payments, depending on whether economies grow rapidly, or are impacted by economic shocks. Even if high growth rates are achieved, a quarter of impoverished countries would still see the share of government income spent on debt payments increase rapidly.'

The group cites the case of Ghana. The IMF and World Bank predict the West African nation's debt payments will increase from 12 per cent of government income in 2014 to 25 per cent by 2023 even if the economy grows by

5.6 per cent a year. If economic growth is less, payments could devour half of government income. Shockingly, this has all occurred since Ghana's debt was cancelled in 2004.[8]

Decades of structural adjustment failed to solve the debt crisis, caused untold suffering for millions of people and led to widening gaps between rich and poor. A 1999 study by the Washington-based group, Development Gap, looked at the impact of SAPs on more than 70 African and Asian countries during the early 1990s. The study concluded that the longer a country operates under structural adjustment, the worse its debt burden becomes. SAPs, Development Gap warned, 'are likely to push countries into a tragic circle of debt, adjustment, a weakened domestic economy, heightened vulnerability and greater debt.'[9]

So we are left with a bizarre and troubling spectacle. In Africa, external debt more than quadrupled after the Bank and the IMF began managing national economies through structural adjustment. According to the UN, in 2004 Zambia had one of the highest rates of HIV/AIDS infection in the world, yet the southern African nation was spending three times as much on debt service as on healthcare. When the country finally completed the HIPC program in April 2005, $4 billion of debt was cancelled. Yet the IMF predicts Zambia's debt payments will triple from $60 million in 2010 to $180 million in 2015.

In Angola, where the average person lives to 52 years of age and 1 in 10 babies dies before their first birthday, over twice as much was spent on debt payments as on healthcare from 2010 to 2014, according to World Bank figures. In the late 1990s, half of all primary-school-age children in Africa were not in school yet governments spent four times more on debt payments than they spent on health and education.

Meanwhile in Latin America, before the debt balloon, Ecuador spent 30 per cent of its revenue on education,

10 per cent on healthcare and 15 per cent servicing its debts. By 2005 the situation was reversed – the nation spent nearly half its income on debt service, 12 per cent on education and just 17 per cent on healthcare. And poverty had increased. When the government opted to channel oil money towards social spending, the IMF and World Bank balked. The Bank delayed and ultimately cancelled an already approved loan as a result of what it described as a 'policy reversal'. In 2007 Ecuador's $17-billion debt had swollen to 40 per cent of its GDP.

SAPs may not have put Third World countries back on a steady economic keel but they have certainly helped undermine democracy in those nations. Critics call it a new form of colonialism.

'Southern debt,' writes political scientist Susan George, 'has relatively little to do with money and finance, and everything to do with the West's continuing exercise of political and economic control. Just think of the advantages: no army, no costly colonial administration, rock-bottom prices for raw materials... It's a dream system and Western powers won't abandon it unless their own outraged citizens – or a far greater unity among debtor nations themselves – oblige them to so do.'[10]

Joseph Stiglitz, former World Bank Chief Economist, is candid about the record of bureaucrats in both the IMF and the World Bank who have eroded the ability of states to govern their own affairs. In an article written shortly after his resignation, Stiglitz said there are 'real risks associated with delegating excessive power to international agencies... The institution can actually become an interest group itself, concerned with maintaining its position and advancing its power.'[11]

Years later, he continued his attack on the limitations of 'market fundamentalism' preached by the IMF and the World Bank. 'The institutions are dominated not just by the wealthiest industrial countries but by the commercial and financial interests in those countries and the policies naturally reflect this... The institutions are not representative of the nations they serve.'[12]

Servicing the national debt has become a major concern in rich and poor countries alike. But especially so in the Global South, where there are far fewer dollars to spend: debt has become a major brake on development.

With the break-up of the Soviet Union and the surging global economy in the early 2000s the triumph of capitalism seemed complete. The great financial meltdown that began in late 2008 shattered that confidence. But memories are short. Deficit fetishism, otherwise known as 'austerity', continues to dominate domestic economic policy across the West, even as unemployment remains stubbornly high.

What is certain is that 'structural adjustment' is an integral part of the modern globalized economy. Indeed, SAPs have a perverse logic when seen through the lens of economic globalization that puts the economy ahead of people. This 'market fundamentalism' has its own basic credo: private corporations should be free to trade, invest and move capital around the globe with a minimum amount of government interference.

But there are fault lines emerging in this elite consensus. People in the Global South are resisting structural adjustment through violent opposition and grassroots organizing. Across Europe millions have protested harsh austerity measures imposed by the 'troika' – the European Commission, the International Monetary Fund and European Central Bank – in return for bailouts to debt-strapped national governments. Protest is simmering across the South, too, not least among the millions uprooted by World Bank mega-projects, particularly the building of huge hydroelectric dams.

Opposition to free trade is on the rise. And in Latin America, governments opposed to – or at least uncomfortable with – the 'Washington Consensus' have been elected in Nicaragua, El Salvador, Uruguay, Paraguay, Argentina, Brazil, Ecuador, Bolivia and Venezuela. The

Lost wealth

A 2014 study by the European Network on Debt and Development found that losses of financial resources by developing countries have been more than twice the amount of new loans and investment since the financial crisis of 2008. The graph shows that lost wealth has been close to 10% of GDP. The main causes are illicit financial flows, profits taken out by foreign investors and lending by developing countries to rich countries.

Inflows vs. losses for developing countries, % GDP (2008-11)

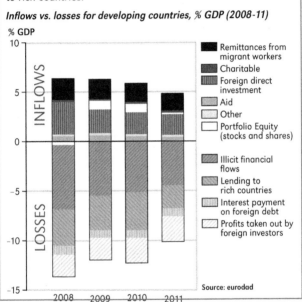

Source: eurodad

one-size-fits-all model of economic globalization is no longer accepted. Religious extremism and the politics of ethnic exclusion (from Palestine to Iraq to India) are turning political costs into military ones. And, as continuing protests against the World Trade Organization and the G8 prove, powerful and unaccountable institutions are coming under pressure from citizens' groups, community activists, students, trade unionists and environmentalists. Many are calling for reform.

Others are going much farther and demanding the outright abolition of these agencies and a complete restructuring of the global economic system.

1 Joseph Hanlon, 'Illegitimate Loans: lenders, not borrowers, are responsible', *Third World Quarterly*, Vol 27, No 2, 2006. **2** 'How Bretton Woods re-ordered the world', *New Internationalist*, No 257, July 1994. **3** 'Debt: the facts', *New Internationalist*, No 312, May 1999. **4** Eric Toussaint, *Your Money or Your Life*, Haymarket, Chicago, 2005. **5** *The Independent*, London, 1 Feb 1999. **6** 'The Multilateral Debt Relief Initiative', *IMF Factsheet*, Sep 2014, nin.tl/IMFonMDRI **7** *Human Development Report 2005*, UNDP, New York, 2005. **8** 'Lending boom threatens to create new debt crises', Jubilee Debt Campaign, Oct 2014, jubileedebt.org.uk **9** 'Conditioning debt relief on adjustment: creating conditions for more indebtedness', Development Gap, Washington 1999. **10** Susan George, *Another World Is Possible If...* , Verso, London/New York, 2004. **11** Jim Lobe, 'Finance: Stiglitz calls for more open debate, less conditionality,' IPS, 30 Nov 1999. **12** Joseph Stiglitz, *Globalization and its Discontents*, Norton, New York/London, 2003.

4 The corporate century

Giant private companies have become the driving force behind economic globalization, wielding more power than many nation-states. Business values of 'efficiency' and 'competition' now dominate the debate on social policy, the public interest and the role of government. The tendency to monopoly, combined with decreasing rates of profit, drives corporate decision-making – with little regard for the social, environmental and economic consequences of those decisions.

The most jarring aspects of travel today are not the cultural differences – though thankfully those still exist – but the commercial similarities. Increasingly, where we travel to feels more and more like the place we just left.

Whether it's Montreal or Mumbai, Beijing or Buenos Aires, globalization has introduced a level of commercial culture which is eerily homogeneous. The glitzy, air-conditioned shopping malls are interchangeable; the same shops sell the same goods. Fast-food restaurants like KFC, Subway, Pizza Hut and Dunkin Donuts are sprinkled around the globe. The emphasis is on high-sugar, high-fat foods – with minor concessions to local tastes. (McDonald's, for example, features a 'paneer salsa wrap' in India, cottage cheese in spicy seasoning, wrapped in a chapati and fried.) KFC has more than 4,200 outlets in China alone.

Young people yearn for the same smartphones, drink the same soft drinks, smoke the same cigarettes, wear identical branded clothing, play the same computer games, watch the same Hollywood films and listen to the same Western pop music.

Welcome to the world of the transnational corporation, a cultural and economic tsunami that is roaring across the globe and replacing the spectacular diversity of human society with a Westernized version of the good life. As corporations market the consumer dream of wealth and glamor, local cultures around the world are marginalized and devalued. Family and community bonds are disintegrating as social relationships are 'commodified' and reduced to what the English social critic Thomas Carlyle called the 'cash nexus' in his 1839 essay, *Chartism*. In the words of Swedish sociologist Helena Norberg-Hodge, there is 'a global monoculture which is now able to disrupt traditional cultures with a shocking speed and finality and which surpasses anything the world has witnessed before.'[1]

Over the past two decades, as global rules regulating the movement of goods and investment have been relaxed, private corporations have expanded their global reach so that their decisions now touch the lives of people in every corner of the world. The vast, earth-straddling companies dominate global trade in everything from computers and pharmaceuticals to insurance, banking and cinema. Their holdings are so numerous and so Byzantine that it is often impossible to trace the chain of ownership. Even so, it is estimated that a third of all trade in the international economy results from shuffling goods between branches of the same corporation.

Some proponents of globalization argue that transnationals are the ambassadors of democracy. They insist that free markets and political freedoms are inextricably bound together and that the introduction of the first will inevitably lead to the second. Unfortunately, the facts don't support their claim. Market economies flourish in some of the world's most autocratic and tyrannical states and transnational corporations have shown surprisingly little interest in, and have had even less effect on, changing political systems. The truth is that corporations follow the money – a nation's political system is largely irrelevant. Saudi Arabia, Malaysia, Indonesia, Pakistan, China, Colombia: all have thriving market systems where big corporations are dominant actors. But none of them can be counted among the world's healthy democracies.

As the US political scientist Benjamin Barber has written: 'Capitalism requires consumers with access to markets and a stable political climate in order to succeed; such conditions may or may not be fostered by democracy, which can be disorderly and even anarchic in its early stages, and which often pursues public goods costly to or at odds with private market imperatives... capitalism does not need or entail democracy.'[2]

Many global corporations now wield more economic power than nation-states. According to 2010 figures from the World Bank and *Forbes* magazine, Wal-Mart took in more revenue than the GDP of South Africa and Greece while Costco's revenue was more than the total GDP of Luxembourg. Exxon, General Electric, Bank of America and Berkshire Hathaway were all in the top 20 global corporations and all had higher revenues than Bangladesh.[3]

An earlier study by the Washington-based Institute for Policy Studies found:

- The world's top 200 corporations accounted for 25 per cent of global economic activity but employed less than one per cent of its workforce.
- Combined sales of the top 200 corporations were 18 times more than the total annual income of 1.2 billion people living in absolute poverty – 24 per cent of the total world population.
- The profits of the top 200 corporations grew 362.4 per cent from 1983 to 1999 while the number of people they employed grew by just 14.4 per cent.[4]

Corporate merger mania

Of course large companies have not just appeared on the scene. They've been with us since the early days of European expansion, when governments routinely granted economic 'adventurers' such as the Hudson

Bay Company and the East India Company the right to control vast swaths of the planet in an attempt to consolidate imperial rule. But there has been nothing in history to match the economic muscle and political clout of today's giants – they grow larger and more powerful by the day. Scarcely a week goes by without another merger between major corporations. The competition for market share over the past two decades has been the catalyst for the biggest shift towards monopoly for a century.

Consolidation has been especially rapid in the tele-communications and media industries, where it is impossible to keep up with the endless shape-shifting. In January 2000, America Online (a distant memory now but then the world's biggest internet provider) announced a $164-billion merger with Time-Warner. That's still the biggest merger of all time but the jockeying amongst telecoms has not stopped. In 2013 Verizon bought Vodafone's 45-per-cent stake in Verizon Wireless for a cool $130 billion, making it the third-largest corporate takeover of all time. That same year Warren Buffet's Berkshire Hathaway holding company snapped up storied ketchup-maker, HJ Heinz, for a paltry $23 billion. In the world of big pharma, the US giant, Pfizer, bought Wyeth for $68 billion in 2009 while the German firm, Merck, engineered a $45-billion merger with Schering Plough, thus becoming the world's second-largest drug company. Meanwhile, in the transport sector, American Airlines acquired US Airways for $11 billion, creating the world's largest airline. A few years earlier, in 2006, both France and Luxembourg fought a losing battle against a $34-billion hostile takeover of Arcelor SA by India-based Mittal. The merger created the world's largest steel company. In 2013 the company had revenues of $72 billion and it produces close to 100 million tons a year.

UN figures indicate that the tendency towards monopoly is growing across a range of industries, including manufacturing, banking and finance, media and entertainment, and communications. But high-profile business marriages are also taking place in older industries like automobiles and transport as well as in primary resources such as mining, forestry and agriculture. The 10 largest corporations in their field now control 86 per cent of the telecommunications

Corporate rule

Huge global corporations are becoming ever more powerful, eroding the regulatory powers of nation-states and riding roughshod over the rights of citizens to determine their own future. Of the top 100 economies, 37 belong to corporations rather than countries, with Wal-Mart the 28th-largest economy in the world.

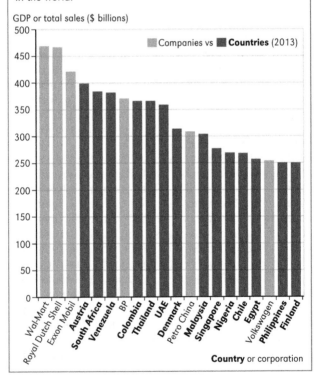

GDP or total sales ($ billions)

Companies vs **Countries** (2013)

Country or corporation

sector, 85 per cent of the pesticides industry, 70 per cent of the computer industry and 35 per cent of the pharmaceutical industry. Between 2003 and 2005, the world's top 10 seed companies increased their control of the world's global seed trade from one-third to one-half.

The recent economic crash cooled corporate merger mania (in 2008 mergers fell by 30 per cent) but not for long. Deal-making has picked up as the global economy has slowly revived. According to Thomson Reuters, the global mergers and acquisitions market in 2013 involved 38,819 deals worth a combined $2,393 billion.[5]

Companies don't do much horse trading when markets and the economy are heading south. So an uptick in mergers and acquisitions is a signal of investor confidence. Stock markets reward the merged corporations with higher share prices on the grounds that the new larger firms will be more 'efficient' and therefore increase company earnings. But what does that notion of 'efficiency' really mean? Mergers squander piles of money but they don't usually produce better services or increase production. The public impact of this very private decision-making process is rarely considered. When corporate giants merge it inevitably leads to job losses and factory closures. From management's perspective this is precisely the point – to bolster the bottom line by trimming costs.

When the Brazilian private equity firm, 3G Capital, and US-based Berkshire Hathaway acquired control of condiments maker, Heinz, in 2013 the writing was on the wall for the 105-year-old factory in Leamington, Ontario. Within months Heinz announced that the plant would be closed: 750 workers lost their jobs as production shifted to the US. The plant was the economic lifeblood of the small town. 'It's impersonal,' the town's deputy mayor, Charlie Wright, told the *Toronto Star*. 'They're looking at the bottom line all the time. They don't look at the impact on people... But numbers have faces, and they have families, and they have schools to go to.'[6] What might

Engulf and Devour, Inc.

Globalization has sparked a frenzy of corporate mergers and acquisitions (M&As). These mega-companies threaten competition and increase the threat of monopoly.

In 2013 more than $2.4 trillion was spent on cross-border M&As. The biggest deals were in telecommunications, energy and real estate.

Top Mergers & Acquisitions, 2013

Target	% sought/ acquired	Buyer	Value ($ millions)
Verizon Wireless	45%	Verizon Communications	130,100
HJ Heinz	100%	Investor Group	27,361
Virgin Media	100%	Liberty Global	25,531
Omnicom	100%	Publicis Groupe SA	19,331
Dell	87%	Investor Group	19,283
NBC/Universal	49%	Comcast	16,700
Portugal Telecom	90%	OiSA	15,717
Life Technologies	100%	Thermo Fisher Scientific	15,368
Westfield Group – Australia/NZ	100%	Westfield Retail Trust	14,009
Shoppers Drug Mart	100%	Loblaw Cos	13,025

be good news for shareholders and money managers is a disaster for both the workers and the community.

Business executives champion the economic 'common sense' of mergers and push for them on the grounds that getting bigger is the only way to compete in a lean-and-mean global marketplace. Size does matter in the cut-throat world of free markets. But fewer companies also increase the tendency towards monopoly by eliminating competition. The easiest way to get rid of competitors is to buy them out. Giant companies also have more power to wring concessions from national and regional governments simply because they are such dominant economic players. All governments are keen to lure investors that promise jobs and growth.

Pushing privatization

The spate of mergers and acquisitions over the last decade reflects the quickly changing nature of the global economy, especially the loosening of foreign-investment regulations and the liberalization of international capital flows. Companies are now freer to compete globally, to grow and expand into overseas markets – and the recent shift to free trade in goods, services and investment capital is furthering this consolidation.

The assumption that competition is good 'in and of itself' is central to the corporate-led model of economic globalization. It's this belief that has led to a worldwide campaign by the economically powerful in favor of privatizing publicly owned enterprises. According to this view, government must be downsized and its role in the provision of public services curtailed. The argument is that governments are inefficient bureaucracies that waste taxpayers' money – so they must be restrained. It's a very human trait to complain, so no wonder this criticism resonates with people of all political stripes. Perhaps that's why, when conservative critics began to bemoan the costs of big government in the 1970s, it didn't take them long to find a sympathetic ear. But instead of streamlining bureaucratic inefficiencies and making government work better, they argued that private business should do the job instead.

This enthusiasm for privatization exploded when Margaret Thatcher came to power in Britain in 1979. State-owned enterprises were auctioned off: the national airline, government-run water, gas, telephone and electric utilities, and the railway system. From 1979 to 1994 the overall number of jobs in the public sector in the UK was reduced from seven million to five million. However, there were few new jobs in the private sector to replace them. And the jobs that were created were in the non-unionized, low-paid, service sector. In the case of British Rail, the 1996 privatization created an inefficient, accident-prone system that depended on massive public subsidies and still had some of the highest rail fares in Europe. In 2014, 20 train lines in Britain were owned or operated by foreign state-owned or state-controlled companies. For a one-off payment to the public purse, the UK government had sold state-owned enterprises that had contributed guaranteed yearly profits to the Treasury.

While much was made of the opportunity for ordinary British people to buy shares in these newly privatized public utilities, the reality was quite different. Nine million UK residents did buy shares but most of them invested less than £1,000 and sold them quickly when they found they could turn a quick profit.

The majority of shares of the former publicly owned companies are now controlled by institutional investors and wealthy individuals. Campaigning journalist Susan George has called privatization 'the alienation and surrender of the product of decades of work by thousands of people to a tiny minority of large investors'.[7]

As governments adopt the private-enterprise model and cut public expenditure, they open areas to market forces that were previously considered the responsibility of the state. After World War Two, in the light of growing socialist sympathies, politicians in the West were convinced by a civic-minded electorate to expand the welfare state, including education, healthcare, unemployment insurance, pensions and other social-security measures. At the same time the state expanded its investment in public infrastructure, building roads, bridges, dams, airports, prisons and hospitals.

Now, with the notion of an 'inefficient' public sector firmly fixed in people's minds, governments are selling off public utilities like water, electricity, airports, even postal services – often because operating budgets have been slashed to ribbons. Even prisons and parks are being privatized as governments pare public expenditure to meet market demands for balanced budgets. All of this has an impact on the public sphere and inevitably contributes to the erosion of shared community. Make no mistake about it, these areas offer tremendous scope for private profits. In the US the total state budget for prisons and jails in 2012 was more than $53 billion.[8]

The new market in public healthcare

Other areas are also being eyed avidly by the private sector. Take state-funded healthcare. In Canada, Australia and Europe, private companies are making major inroads into publicly financed healthcare as deficit-conscious politicians slash budgets. This systematic de-funding shows no sign of slowing down as governments seek to reduce public debt in the midst of a weak economy. In the US, where the Obama administration eventually passed a watered-down Affordable Care Act, private insurance companies still hold sway. They have the power to raise premiums to increase profits and have more influence on decision-making than doctors or patients.

At the international level, the General Agreement on Trade in Services (GATS), administered by the World Trade Organization (WTO), was created in 1994. One of the goals of the GATS is to classify public health as a 'service industry', eventually opening the door to full-scale commercialization.

The for-profit health sector in the US has been actively lobbying to pave the way for overseas expansion. A document by the US Coalition of Services Industries in November 1999 suggested that Washington push the WTO to 'encourage more privatization' and to provide 'market access and national treatment, allowing provision of all healthcare services cross-border'. The ultimate goal was clearly spelled out: to allow 'majority foreign ownership of healthcare facilities'. The logic of the market is already intruding into the debate around healthcare policy. But the great fear for defenders of state-funded healthcare in Europe, Canada and elsewhere is that privatization will lead to a two-tier system. Wealthy patients jump the queue and receive state-of-the-art care while the rest of us make do with poorly equipped, underfunded hospitals, long waiting lists and overworked doctors, nurses and technicians.

Privatization has been strongly endorsed by both the World Bank and the IMF and is a standard ingredient in any 'structural adjustment' prescription. It is based on the notion that governments have no business in the marketplace and that the least government is the best government. Despite strong criticism of its policies, the Bank remains wedded to privatization.

Its Private Sector Development Strategy, released in February 2002, reinforces what the Bank calls 'policy-based lending to promote privatization'. The initiative seeks to expand the Bank's business-friendly division, the International Finance Corporation (IFC), whose role is to open doors for private companies, both foreign and domestic. The emphasis is on increasing the role of private business in the service sector: water, sanitation, electricity, education and healthcare.

Take the case of water. Since the 1980s the World Bank has been the biggest backer of water privatization in the developing world, with the IFC as its main channel for loans and financing. Yet its own data shows a 34-per-cent failure rate for private water and sewerage contracts between 2000 and 2010.[9]

How much room do poor nations have to reject or shape adjustment policies which are presented to them by the Bank or the IMF as conditions of borrowing? The answer is: virtually none. The Bank and the IMF have been enforcing market fundamentalism for decades. Often privatization is a 'condition' for release of aid funds. They jointly launched the Heavily Indebted Poor Countries Initiative (HIPC) in 1996. To qualify for debt relief under the program Southern nations must fall into line. According to an Oxfam UK report, debt relief to Honduras under the HIPC was delayed for six months when the IMF demanded more progress on electricity privatization.[10] As a result of this pressure, the ability of governments to make sovereign policy decisions on behalf of their citizens is compromised.

Largely due to this arm-twisting, state assets have been auctioned off across the developing world and the former Soviet Union. In Russia, the transition to private ownership was riddled with corruption. Former Communist Party *apparatchiks* wound up in control of most state assets while billions hemorrhaged out of the country into numbered Swiss bank accounts. According to historian and investigative journalist Paul Klebnikov, the country suffered its worst economic decline since the Nazi invasion of 1942: 'There was a 42-per-cent decline in GDP. The population was impoverished. Mortality rates rocketed and the Russian state was essentially bankrupt.'[11] Klebnikov put the blame for this 'shock therapy' squarely on Western institutions. In 2002, he told *Multinational Monitor*: 'Governments such as the American government at the time, august Western universities such as Harvard, and international financial institutions like the IMF, bear significant responsibility and must answer for their complicity in creating this whole catastrophe.'[12] The oligarchs who profited from Russia's privatization plan were not amused. Klebnikov was murdered in Moscow in 2004.

Across the Global South, privatization has been bedeviled by corruption, regulatory failure and corporate bullying. In the energy sector, for example, companies are often reluctant to invest in power projects without a guaranteed return. Enter the 'power-purchase agreement' – a legal sleight of hand which requires a publicly owned electricity distributor to buy power from private producers at a fixed price in US dollars for up to 30 years – even if demand swoons and the power is not used. In India, the Maharashtra State Electricity Board (MSEB) was fleeced by the now-disgraced corporation Enron and its $920-million Dabhol power plant. At one point, after renegotiating the power-purchase deal, the MSEB was obliged to pay Enron $30 billion a year. Indian critics called the deal 'the most massive fraud in the country's history'. Indian novelist and activist Arundhati Roy says that the MSEB was forced to cut production from its own plants to buy power from Dabhol and hundreds of small industries had to close because they couldn't afford the expensive power. 'Privatization,' Roy writes, 'is presented as being the only alternative to an inefficient, corrupt state. In fact, it's not a choice at all... [it's a] mutually profitable business contract between the private company (preferably foreign) and the ruling elite.'[13]

The problem with foreign direct investment

In addition to selling off public assets, governments are desperate to attract private investment. But investment by foreign corporations is by no means a guarantee of economic progress.

A large chunk of foreign direct investment (FDI) is used to buy out state firms, purchase equity in local companies or finance mergers and acquisitions. Cross-

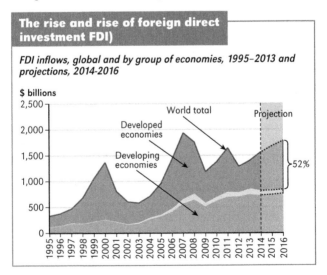

The rise and rise of foreign direct investment FDI)

FDI inflows, global and by group of economies, 1995–2013 and projections, 2014-2016

$ billions

World total
Projection
Developed economies
Developing economies
52%

border mergers and acquisitions account for about 80 per cent of total foreign direct investment yearly. Little of this ends up in new productive activity and there is almost always a net loss of jobs as a result of downsizing after mergers are completed. Increased investment from abroad can also cause a net drain on foreign exchange as transnational companies remit profits to their overseas headquarters. If a foreign corporation produces mainly for local markets, and especially if it edges out local suppliers rather than replacing imports, it may actually worsen balance-of-payments problems.

It's not 'how much' but 'what kind' of FDI that matters. National governments need to select foreign investment that will produce net benefits for their citizens and reject those investments whose overall impact will be negative. Foreign investment can make a positive contribution to national development – but only if it is channelled into productive rather than speculative activities. Unfortunately, the ability to shape foreign investment is dwindling as free-trade arrangements and bilateral trade agreements effectively tie the hands of states which agree to them, inevitably compromising government sovereignty.

Nonetheless, most Southern governments are anxious to attract investment from global corporations – despite the concern about corporate power and unethical behavior. After all, transnational companies are extremely skilled at delivering the goods. They are at the cutting edge of technological innovation and they can introduce new management and marketing strategies. And it's generally the case that wages and working conditions are better in foreign subsidiaries than in local companies.

But overseas investors don't automatically favor countries simply because they've loosened regulations on profit remittances or corporate taxes. The big money predictably goes where it's safest and where the potential for profit is greatest. Most direct investment is concentrated in a small number of developing countries.

According to UNCTAD's *World Investment Report 2013* the bulk of investment in the Global South went to a handful of countries – Brazil, Mexico, India, Indonesia and especially China.[14]

Transnationals are also major players in research and development (R&D). They account for close to half of global R&D expenditure, eclipsing many governments. The world's largest R&D spenders are concentrated in a few industries – information technology hardware, the automotive industry, pharmaceuticals and biotechnology.

Investors crave stability, which is why nearly 60 per cent of all foreign investment goes to industrial countries. The US, Britain, Australia, Ireland, France, Canada and Spain receive the lion's share. Yet even in the West corporations have the upper hand, trading off one nation against another to see which can offer the most lucrative investment incentives. Governments drain the public purse in their attempts to buy jobs from private investors. Tax holidays, interest-free loans, research grants, training schemes, unhindered profit remittances and publicly funded sewers, roads and utilities are among the mix of 'incentives' that companies now expect in return for opening up a new factory or office.

The largest transnationals call themselves 'global firms', which might lead one to believe that they are stateless, disembodied entities toiling for the good of humankind. The truth is more complex. There are few giant companies that are truly stateless; most are firmly tied to one national home base. Bill Gates' Microsoft is identifiably American. Total is French, Siemens is German, Vodafone is British and the giant aerospace conglomerate Embraer is Brazilian. But nationality is disposable when profits entice. Companies may wrap themselves in the national flag when lobbying local governments for tax breaks, start-up grants or other goodies. But their allegiances are fickle – and quickly diverted if opportunities for profit appear greater elsewhere. The fact that transnational corporations are relatively footloose means they can move to where costs are cheapest – and play off one government against another in the process. Examples fill the business press daily. Bombardier, a Canadian company that had received millions in government subsidies, announced in 2005 that it was exporting 500 highly paid, skilled jobs to India, China and Mexico, claiming that it needed to 'return to profitability by reducing operating costs'.[15] Companies also look to escape taxes whenever possible. In September 2014 the Obama administration moved to close a loophole on 'tax inversion'. This legal dodge allowed companies to buy a foreign rival then relocate the head office outside the US to take advantage of lower taxes. Washington's move came as fast-food giant Burger King was attempting to 'invert' to Toronto in a deal with the iconic Canadian coffee-and-donuts chain, Tim Hortons.

This political power – to pull up stakes, lay off workers, move management and shift production – is a powerful bargaining chip that business can use to squeeze greater concessions from job-hungry governments.

One of the corporate sector's greatest political victories in recent decades has been to beat down corporate taxes. In Britain, the corporate tax rate fell from 52 per cent in 1979 to 30 per cent in 2000 and Prime Minister Tony Blair boasted that British business was subject to fewer strictures than corporations in the US. By 2014, the UK corporation tax rate had plunged still further to just 21 per cent, way below the US rate of 40 per cent and the French rate of 33 per cent and the Canadian rate of 26.5 per cent.[16]

Corporate tax rates have declined in virtually every OECD country over the last two decades as governments rely more and more on personal income taxes and sales taxes for revenues. (Between 2000 and 2011, debt-strapped Greece pared its rate from 40 per cent to 20 per cent.) In 1950 corporate taxes in the US accounted for 30 per cent of government funds; today they account for less than 12 per cent. In Canada, the effective federal corporate tax rate was cut from 28 per cent in 2000 to 15 per cent in 2012. Meanwhile, corporate income taxes accounted for just 7.85 per cent of government revenues, down from an average 11 per cent in the 1960s and 1970s. The main point is that corporations play one country against another to reduce taxes and increase profits. But they also employ scores of tax lawyers and accountants to ensure they pay as little as possible.

Their sheer size, wealth and power mean that transnationals and the business sector in general have been able to structure the public debate on social issues and the role of government in a way that benefits their own interests. They have used their louder voices and political clout to build an effective propaganda machine and to boost what the Italian political theorist Antonio Gramsci called their 'cultural hegemony'. Through sophisticated public relations, media manipulation and friends in high places, the orthodoxy of corporate-led globalization has become the 'common sense' approach to running a country. This radical paradigm shift has occurred in the short space of 40 years – an extraordinary accomplishment by a cadre of rightwing thinktanks, radical entrepreneurs and their academic supporters.

The more our lives become entangled in the market, the more the ideology of profit before people becomes accepted. A corporation's ultimate responsibility is not to society but to its shareholders, as Chief Executive Officers (CEOs) constantly reassure their investors at annual general meetings. Enhanced value for shareholders drives corporate decision-making – without regard for the social, environmental and economic consequences of those decisions. The public is the loser. Unless social obligations are imposed on companies, the business agenda will continue to ride roughshod over national and community interests. Capitalism and the public good are not necessarily congruent.

Impacts of NAFTA

The North American Free Trade Agreement (NAFTA) was one of the first regional economic pacts developed to further corporate globalization. The Washington-based non-governmental organization, Public Citizen, has documented a steady movement of US companies to cheap labor zones in Mexico and the direct loss of hundreds of thousands of jobs since NAFTA came into effect in 1995.

The activist group cites the example of the jeans maker Guess? Inc which, according to the *Wall Street Journal*, cut the percentage of its clothes sewn in Los Angeles from 97 per cent prior to NAFTA to 35 per cent two years later. In that period the company relocated five sewing factories to Mexico and others to Peru and Chile. More than 1,000 workers in Los Angeles lost their jobs. According to the Washington-based Economic Policy Institute, the deal eliminated nearly 880,000 jobs, most in high-paying manufacturing, while the ones that replaced them were low-paid, non-unionized service jobs. NAFTA also had a negative effect on the wages of US workers whose jobs were not relocated. They are now in direct competition with skilled, educated Mexican workers who work for a dollar or two an hour – or less. As a result their bargaining power with employers has been substantially eroded. NAFTA was supposed to solve this problem by raising Mexican living standards and wages. Sadly, that has not happened. Instead, workers on both sides of the Rio Grande have suffered.

NAFTA's labor side-agreement was supposed to cushion workers but it didn't work out that way. Instead, labor protections built into Mexico's legal system have been attacked as obstacles to investment. In 2002, Mexican President Vicente Fox announced he would support the World Bank's recommendations to scrap most of Mexico's Federal Labor Law – eliminating mandatory severance pay and the 40-hour week. Mexico's historic (though not always enforced) ban on strike-breaking and guarantees of healthcare and housing would be gutted as well.

The policy of encouraging foreign investment at all cost has also led to the wholesale privatization of Mexican industry and the effects have been devastating. While three-quarters of the workforce belonged to unions three decades ago, less than 30 per cent does today. Private owners reduced the membership of the railway workers' union from 90,000 to 36,000.

Since 1994, half a million Mexicans have left their country every year. The recent world crisis has led to more displacement. The economy shrank by more than 10 per cent and 700,000 jobs were lost from October 2008 to May 2009. In response, President Felipe Calderón prescribed a two-per-cent tax on food and medicine, together with sharp hikes in the price of electricity, gas and water.

During the last two decades, the income of Mexican workers has lost 76 per cent of its purchasing power. Under pressure from foreign lenders, the government ended subsidies on the prices of basic necessities – including gasoline, electricity, bus fares, tortillas and milk – all of which have risen drastically. In 2012, an estimated 54 million people lived in poverty and 12 million in extreme poverty. Before the crash of 2007-8, the country's independent union federation, the National Union of Workers, claimed that more than nine million people were out of work – a quarter of the workforce.

Well before NAFTA, the disparity between US and Mexican wages was growing. Mexican salaries were a third of those in the US in the 1970s. They are now less than an eighth. It is this disparity which both impoverishes Mexican workers and acts as a magnet drawing production from the US. By exacerbating these trends, NAFTA forced working communities in Canada, the US and Mexico to ask some basic questions.[17]

As corporations gain the upper hand, fear of job losses and the resulting social devastation have created a downward pressure on environmental standards and social programs – what critics of corporate power call 'a race to the bottom'.

NAFTA is one of more than 3,000 trade and investment treaties around the world. Almost all of these carry provisions that empower corporations while restricting national governments from interfering with the 'wisdom' of the market. Business is constantly pushing to expand the freedom to trade and invest, unhindered by either government regulations or social obligations.

The fights against the MAI and TTIP

The Multilateral Agreement on Investment (MAI) was one infamous example of the attempt by big business to remake the world in its image.

The public has been wary of the WTO for some time. But the MAI flew under the radar until activists stumbled across it in 1997. After the WTO was created in 1994, the globe's major corporations began to put together a plan for codifying the rules of world trade in a way that would give them the upper hand. They found it in the MAI. The agreement was drafted by the International Chamber of Commerce (a 'professional association' of the world's largest companies) and presented to the rich-nation OECD members for discussion and, it was assumed, rubber-stamp approval.

Majority World governments were suspicious of the MAI; many saw it as 'a throwback to colonial-era economics'. But, with the weight of the OECD behind it, supporters reckoned it would be speedily adopted as an official WTO document.

Delegates from OECD countries began discussing the MAI in early 1995 behind closed doors. By early 1997 most of the treaty was on paper and the public was none the wiser. In fact, most politicians in the OECD's 29 member countries weren't even aware of the negotiations. When activists in Canada got their hands on a copy of the MAI and began sending it around the world via the internet, the full scope of the document became clear.

Essentially the proposed agreement set out to give private companies the same legal status as nation-states in all countries that signed on. But, more importantly, it also laid out a clear set of rules so corporations would be able to defend their new rights against the objections of sovereign governments. The MAI was so overwhelmingly biased towards the interests of transnational companies that critics were quick to label it 'the corporate rule treaty'.

For example, under MAI provisions corporations could sue governments for passing laws that might reduce their potential profits. They could make their case in secret with no outside interest groups involved and the decision would be binding. The MAI also allowed foreign investors to challenge public funding of social programs as a distortion of free markets and the 'level playing field'. If a government chose to privatize a state-owned industry, it could no longer give preference to domestic buyers. In addition, governments would be forbidden to demand that foreign investment benefit local communities or the national economy. They could not demand domestic content, local hiring, affirmative action, technology transfer or anything else in return for allowing foreign companies to exploit publicly owned resources. And there were to be no limits on profit repatriation.

Once the text became public, citizens' groups around the world began vigorous education campaigns on the damaging impact of the MAI. Two influential activists, Tony Clarke and Maude Barlow, summed up the feelings of citizens' groups everywhere. 'The MAI', they wrote, 'would provide foreign investors with new and substantive rights with which they could challenge government programs, policies and laws all over the world.'[18]

In a few months, public anxiety about the deal came to a head. In France, Australia, Canada and the US, politicians at all levels were drawn into the debate and governments were forced to enter 'reservations' to protect themselves from certain of the MAI's provisions. By the May 1998 deadline it was clear that the talks were at a standstill and that public opposition had torpedoed further progress on the Agreement.

This was a clear victory for a growing international citizens' movement. But the end of the MAI did not spell the end of the corporate agenda for a global investment treaty. The focus would now shift to both regional and country-to-country trade agreements where corporations could lobby for the MAI-like investment provisions.

Since then we've seen major new initiatives like the Transatlantic Trade and Investment Partnership (TTIP) between the US and the EU, the Comprehensive Economic and Trade Agreement (CETA) deal between Canada and the EU, and the Trans-Pacific Partnership (TPP) nego-tiations involving 12 nations strung along the Pacific Rim. These deals all bow to investor rights by including a clause to resolve what are called 'investor-state dispute settlements' (ISDS). NAFTA has a similar provision and the MAI was to include an ISDS mechanism too. This point is to allow corporations to sue governments if they stand in the way of open investment. In other words, business knows best and politics must not be allowed to get in the way.

In an open letter to UNCTAD, more than 250 non-governmental organizations wrote: 'Through the dispute process, states' regulatory efforts in the areas of health, environment and climate change, financial stability, water, labor rights and agriculture, among other areas, have been challenged, with billions of dollars of taxpayer money already awarded to corporations, and with many billions more still pending.' The consequences are clear enough. Researcher Scott Sinclair points out that, as a result of similar ISDS provisions in NAFTA, 'Canada has already paid out more than $170 million in damages and is facing billions of dollars in current claims related to resource management, energy and pharmaceutical patents'.[19]

The downward pressure on wages and social programs caused by economic globalization is compounded by the rise of free trade zones (FTZs), which now exist in more than 135 countries – there are more than 3,000 FTZs around the globe – from Malaysia and the Philippines to El Salvador, Mexico and even socialist Cuba. These officially sanctioned sites exist almost as separate countries, offering their corporate clients minimal taxes, lax environmental regulations, cheap labor and low overheads.

The dangers of overproduction

In their urgent need to grow, corporations have ignored a fundamental aspect of capitalist production: over-capacity. It was Henry Ford, one of the pioneers of mass production, who realized 80 years ago the inherent dilemma of replacing labor with machines and then paying the remaining workers poverty-level wages. You could produce a lot of cars but in the end you would have no-one who could afford to buy them: too many goods and too few buyers. Today, sophisticated improvements in manufacturing equipment have boosted productivity while destroying millions of jobs and curbing wage growth. Henry Ford's own automobile sector is a case in point. One major reason for the massive restructuring in that industry over the past decade is over-capacity, estimated at more than 30 per cent worldwide. According to *The Economist*, the global auto industry can produce 20 million more vehicles a year than the market can absorb. Production is shifting to low-wage countries like Mexico, which was the world's eighth-largest carmaker in 2014. Companies like Ford and Nissan have pledged to invest billions there in the future. China is still the world's largest car maker, with a quarter of global production – followed by the US, Japan, Germany and South Korea. But this may change. The average manufacturing wage in China at $3.50 per hour is now higher than the $2.70 per hour in Mexico. (Car workers in North America make between $25 and $30 an hour.)

There is a global over-capacity in everything from shoes and steel to clothing and electronic goods. One estimate puts the excess manufacturing capacity in China alone at more than 40 per cent. As industries consolidate to cut losses, factories are closed but output remains the same or even increases. This produces falling rates of profit, which in turn drives industry to look for further efficiencies. One tack is to continue to cut labor costs – which helps the bottom line initially but actually dampens global demand over time. Another is the merger-and-acquisition route – cut costs by consolidating production, closing factories and laying off workers. However, this too is self-defeating in the long run since it also inevitably reduces demand.

The real danger of this overproduction is 'deflation'. Instead of a steady rise in employment and relatively stable prices for commodities and manufactured goods, deflation is a downward spiral of both prices and wages. In economic terms, the formula is simple: capacity exceeds demand, prices fall, unemployment rises and wages are forced down farther.

In the 1930s, the result was a resounding and destructive economic crash which saw plants close and millions of workers made redundant. This catastrophe was reversed only when factories boosted production of armaments and other supplies for the Second World War. So far deflation has been kept at bay in the 21st century by making the US economy the 'consumer of last resort'. According to the IMF, the US has provided about half the growth in total world demand since 1988. The US may still be recovering from the 2008 recession but the dollar is still vastly overvalued and its economy continues to suck in cheap imports from the rest of the world. Every day, Americans borrow $3 billion from foreigners – a form of 'vendor financing' – to pay for imports and to keep domestic interest rates low. The result is colossal domestic debt and record trade deficits. In 2013, the US trade deficit was $472 billion, down from $700 billion in 2007 but still nearly three per cent of GDP. China's trade surplus with the United States increased from $11 billion in 1990 to a whopping $298 billion in 2012 – the country's largest bilateral deficit.

In an era of globalized free markets, all countries try to fight their way to prosperity by boosting exports. That's partly because traditional Keynesian methods of stimulating domestic growth by 'priming the pump' had fallen into disfavor prior to the collapse of the global economy in 2008. And few countries have either the inclination or the political will to direct domestic savings toward investment in the local market. Instead, all nations look outwards; international trade is seen as the ticket to economic growth. The financial meltdown saw a dramatic turnaround in world trade. Manufactured exports worldwide fell by half or more from late 2007 to mid-2009, the first time world trade had contracted since 1945. A few years earlier, in 2004, according to the WTO, the value of world merchandise trade rose by 21 per cent to $8.88 trillion while trade in services jumped by 16 per cent to $2.10 trillion. Yet, as UNDP's 2005 *Human Development Report* pointed out: 'After more than two decades of rapid trade growth, high-income countries representing 15 per cent of the world's population still account for two-thirds of world exports – a modest decline from the position in 1980.'

The success of any country vis-à-vis another depends on how competitively (ie how cheaply) it can price its goods in the world market. This competition inevitably means cutting costs and the easiest costs to cut are wages. But, as we have already seen, cheap labor exports inevitably backfire by undermining domestic purchasing power and depressing domestic demand. Simply put: workers earn less so they have less to spend. As University of Ottawa economist Michel Chossudovsky notes: 'The expansion of exports from developing countries is predicated on the contraction of internal purchasing power. Poverty is an input on the supply side.'[20]

Over the past 15 years, the UN has documented a steady shift of global income from wages to profits. Even so, investors are no longer satisfied with five or six per cent annual returns. Trade and investment barriers started to crumble as economic globalization took hold. But corporations, banks and other major investors were looking for quicker ways of maximizing their returns. The solution was at hand. From the 'real' economy of manufacturing and commodity production, investors turned to the world of international finance. Speculation and gambling in international money markets seemed easier than competing for fewer and fewer paying customers in the old goods and services economy. Welcome to the era of the 'global casino'.

1 Helena Norberg-Hodge 'The march of the monoculture', *The Ecologist*, Vol 29, No 2, May/Jun 1999. **2** Benjamin R Barber, *Jihad vs McWorld*, Ballantine Books, New York, 1995. **3** Comparison of the World's 25 Largest Corporations with the GDP of Selected Countries: 2010', Global Policy Forum, globalpolicy.org **4** Sarah Anderson and Jon Cavanagh, *Top 200: the Rise of Corporate Global Power*, Institute for Policy Studies, Washington, 2000. **5** Mergers & Acquisitions 2013, Thomson Reuters, nin.tl/MandA2013 **6** Jennifer Wells, 'Loss of Heinz and ketchup-making devastates Leamington', *Toronto Star*, 23 May 2014. **7** Susan George, 'A short history of neo-liberalism', paper presented to the conference on Economic sovereignty in a globalizing world, Bangkok, March 1999. **8** Fact Sheet: 'Trends in US Correction', The Sentencing Project, sentencingproject.org **9** Anna Lappé, 'World Bank wants water privatized, despite risks', *Aljazeera America*, 17 April 2014. **10** K Bayliss, 'Privatization and poverty', Jan 2002, http://idpm.man.ac.uk/crc/ **11** 'The theft of the century', *Multinational Monitor*, Jan/Feb 2002. **12** 'Privatization and the Looting of Russia', *Multinational Monitor*, Jan/Feb 2002. **13** Arundhati Roy, *Power politics*, South End Press, Boston, 2001. **14** 'FDI Inflows, Top 20 host economies 2013', UNCTAD. **15** '90 more Downsview plan jobs may flee', *Toronto Star*, 27 Sep 2005. **16** nin.tl/corptaxrates **17** Excerpted from David Bacon, 'Up for grabs', *New Internationalist*, No 374, Dec 2004. **18** This description of the battle against the MAI owes much to Tony Clarke and Maude Barlow, *MAI Round 2: new global and internal threats to Canadian sovereignty*, Stoddart, 1998. **19** 'Making Sense of the CETA', Canadian Centre for Policy Alternatives, Sep 2014, policyalternatives.ca **20** Michel Chossudovsky, *The globalization of poverty*, Third World Network, 1997.

5 Global casino

The deregulation of the finance sector, coupled with the digital revolution, has sparked a surge in the international flow of capital. Uncontrolled speculation has eclipsed long-term productive investment and poses a huge threat to the stability of the global economy. Recent financial crises, including the crash of 2008, have caused suffering for millions and confirm the need for urgent action to control the money markets and rein in currency traders.

The acceleration of economic globalization is dramatically altering life for people around the world. As wealth increases for a minority, disparities between rich and poor widen and the assault on our planet's natural resources speeds up.

But the biggest and most dangerous change over the past 35 years has been in the area of global finance. The volume of worldwide foreign-exchange transactions has exploded as country after country has lowered barriers to foreign investment. In 1980, the daily average of foreign-exchange trading totalled $80 billion. In 2013, the Geneva-based Bank for International Settlements (BIS) estimated that more than $5,300 billion changes hands every day on global currency markets. That's an astounding $1,934,500 billion a year, more than 100 times greater than the total value of all goods and services traded globally during the same period. This is an unimaginable sum of money.[1] But it is all the more stunning when you realize that most of this investment has almost nothing to do with producing real goods or services for real people. Less than five per cent of all currency trading is linked to actual trade. The rest is speculative profit-seeking.

The world of international finance is technically arcane but the main point is easily understood. The goal is to make money – the end-use of the investment is relevant only to the extent that it is profitable. As growth in the real economy declines due to overcapacity and shrinking wages worldwide, speculative investment has grown. Money chasing money has eclipsed productive investment as the engine of the global economy.

There are very few controls on the movement of international capital. Yet the predominant view of the Bretton Woods institutions, the giant global banks and private corporations is that the world needs more financial liberalization, not less.

Others are not so sure. They're more inclined to believe what Keynes wrote in his 1936 book *The General Theory of Employment, Interest and Money*. 'Speculators may do no harm as bubbles on a steady stream of enterprise. But the position is serious when enterprise becomes the bubble on a whirlpool of speculation.'

The rules for running the global economy, laid down at the 1944 Bretton Woods Conference, specifically sought to rein in finance capital and contain it within national borders. Keynes, Britain's chief delegate at the gathering, warned that unregulated flows of capital would remove power from elected politicians and put it into the hands of the rich investors – whose ultimate allegiance was to their own self-interest.

Short-term speculation wreaks havoc

Today that self-interest is creating global havoc. Since governments in the industrialized countries began to deregulate financial markets in 1979, short-term speculation has become the single largest component in the flow of international investment. Managers of billion-dollar hedge funds, mutual funds and pension plans move money in and out of countries at lightning speed based on fractional differences in exchange rates. This volatile flow of currency is almost completely detached from the physical economy. For every dollar that is needed to facilitate the trade in real goods, nine dollars is gambled in foreign-exchange markets.

Critics of corporate-led globalization charge that unregulated flows of capital pose a major threat to the stability of the world economy, turning it into a 'global casino'. This free flow of capital has also had a direct political impact, leaving national governments hostage to market forces. Any departure from the received wisdom is instantly punished. Without regulation, investors can pull up stakes at a moment's notice. Governments are hesitant to introduce laws that might upset investors and cause capital to flee, taking potential jobs with them and possibly sparking economic chaos. This threat is a powerful brake on national sovereignty, reducing the political space for governments to control their own economic destiny. Such is the power of finance capital today.

The development of sophisticated computerized communications, combined with a global push for financial deregulation in the early 1980s, opened the doors to speculative investment. A decade later, the World Bank, the IMF and the US Treasury preached the gospel of liberal financial markets, pressing Third World governments to open up their stock markets and financial services (banks, insurance companies, bond dealers and the like).

As noted, the Bretton Woods agreements specifically sought to limit the movement of finance capital and contain it within national borders. Article VI of the original IMF Articles of Agreement allows members 'to exercise such controls as are necessary to regulate international capital movements'. But free-market ideologues dismissed these concerns as old-fashioned and irrelevant in the modern world.

Under pressure from what Columbia University economist Jagdish Bhagwati calls the 'Wall Street/ Treasury complex', governments in the early 1980s began to dismantle controls on the flow of capital and cross-border profits. Bhagwati argues that lax capital controls serve the 'self-interest' of financiers by enlarging the area in which they can make money.[2]

At the same time the financial-services industry itself underwent an unprecedented revolution, sparking a wave of mergers, acquisitions and overseas expansion. In most countries, banks, trust companies, insurance companies and investment brokerages were given the right to fight for each other's business and to compete across international borders. This level of deregulation had not been witnessed in Western countries since the Depression of the 1930s.

The boom in the finance industry was closely linked to the digital revolution. Computerization means currency traders can move millions of dollars around the world instantly with a few taps on a computer keyboard. Investors profit from minute fluctuations in the price of currencies. The result is what Filipino activist Walden Bello calls global arbitrage – a game where 'capital moves from one market to another, seeking profits... by taking advantage of interest-rate differentials, targeting gaps between nominal currency values and the "real" currency values, and short-selling in stocks – borrowing shares to artificially inflate share values, then selling.'[3] Volatility is central to this high-tech world of instant millions and Bello, among others, argues that it has become the driving force of the global capitalist system as a whole. According to the *Wall Street Journal*, 'Increased activity by smaller banks, hedge funds and computer-driven trading programs that can buy and sell currencies in milliseconds' has fuelled speculative trends. As a result, says the BIS, the volume of currency trading from these sources ballooned by 53 per cent from 2010 to 2013.[4]

Financial crises proliferate

Besides speculating in foreign-exchange markets, money managers may also choose to put their funds into direct investment or portfolio investment. Foreign direct investment (FDI) – which tends to be stable and more long-term – occurs when foreigners buy equity in local companies, purchase existing companies or actually

Riding the whirlpool

More than $5 trillion ($5,000 billion) changes hands daily on global currency markets.

- An estimated 95% of all forex deals are short-term speculation; more than 80% are completed in less than a week and 40% in less than two days.
- From 2010 to 2013 the daily volume of forex transactions increased by 32% from $4 trillion to $5.3 trillion. Three days of foreign exchange turnover is enough to cover world trade for a year. The US dollar was dominant, accounting for $4.6 trillion or 87% of the daily total in 2013.
- It is estimated that a 'Robin Hood' tax of just 0.5% on all financial transactions would discourage speculators and raise more than $400 billion yearly for global development. Transaction taxes already exist in Hong Kong, Mumbai, Seoul, Johannesburg and Tapei.

Rate of growth of foreign exchange markets

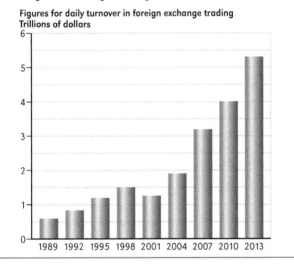

Figures for daily turnover in foreign exchange trading
Trillions of dollars

start up a new factory or business. Foreign portfolio investment (FPI) – which is typically more volatile – is when foreigners buy shares in the local stock market. The trouble begins because portfolio investors have few ties to bind them to the countries in which their funds are invested. In the current global system, where liberalized financial markets are the norm, there are no constraints to prohibit investors from selling when they've turned a quick profit or from exiting at the first signs of financial difficulties.

UNCTAD documented the shift from FDI to FPI during the 1990s. According to its 1998 *World Investment Report*, FPI accounted for a third of all private investment in developing countries from 1990 to 1997. And in some countries, like Argentina, Brazil, Mexico, Thailand and South Korea, portfolio investment actually outpaced direct investment. Portfolio investment is also funnelled through offshore tax havens and other 'friendly' regulatory regimes. For example, FPI in Luxembourg in 2012 was $2.3 trillion. In the Cayman Islands the figure was $2 trillion – a thousand times bigger than the nation's relatively tiny GDP of $2 billion. In the same year, FPI also exceeded GDP in Aruba, Vanuatu, Malta, Guernsey and the Isle of Man.[5]

UNCTAD notes that increasing FPI can signal a more volatile global economy because portfolio investors are 'attracted not so much by the prospect of long-term growth as by the prospect of immediate gain'. Thus they are prone to herd behavior, which can lead to 'massive withdrawals' in a crisis.

And there have been plenty of such crises. One 2002 study from the US National Bureau of Economic Research found that there were 48 financial crises around the world from 1949 to 1971 and 139 from 1973 to 1997 in the era of hyper-deregulation. Research by IMF economists Luc Laeven and Fabián Valencia found there were 146 banking crises, 218 currency crises and 66 sovereign debt crises from 1970 to 2011, noting that these types of financial crises often overlap.

Since the 1997 meltdown in Asia, there have been financial crises in Russia, Brazil, Turkey and Argentina. And of course, the global crash of 2008 was a watershed. The following year banking crises emerged in Denmark,

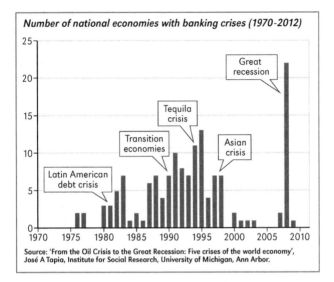

Number of national economies with banking crises (1970-2012)

Great recession

Tequila crisis

Transition economies

Asian crisis

Latin American debt crisis

Source: 'From the Oil Crisis to the Great Recession: Five crises of the world economy', José A Tapia, Institute for Social Research, University of Michigan, Ann Arbor.

Germany, Greece, Ireland, Mongolia and Ukraine; then in Kazakhstan in 2010 and in Nigeria and Spain in 2011. Each of these required active intervention by international financial institutions and national governments to keep the world system from collapsing.

We are still living with the legacy of the 2008 collapse. Details of the 'sub-prime mortgage crisis' are now well known. A combination of greed and speculation by banks, mortgage companies and investment firms led to a colossal housing bubble in the US and Europe. Cheap mortgages triggered a frenzy of activity and a surging real-estate market. It was a classic 'bubble' mentality, with everyone hoping to make a quick buck. US bankers offered sub-prime mortgages to buyers who were living from pay check to pay check. Exotic new financial instruments were invented ('credit default swaps' and 'collateralized debt obligations'). Cheap mortgages were bundled, sold and resold, spreading the risk – and the potential damage – across the global banking system. When US interest rates were raised to stifle inflation, mortgage payments became too expensive for low-income homeowners, forcing many into default. As the market collapsed, house prices fell. Many people with sub-prime mortgages ended up owing more than their house was worth. As a result, tens of thousands of lenders had no way of recouping their loans. Rising defaults pushed many US mortgage companies into bankruptcy. But the 'toxic assets' also infected overseas banks that had joined the hyper-inflated US market. With losses mounting and fear spreading, the whole system went into shock and began to shut down. Confidence disappeared. Banks refused to lend to each other; money markets froze; credit dried up and economic growth ground to a halt.

The bursting of the US sub-prime housing bubble brought untold calamity to millions of people around the world. Families lost their homes, their jobs, their dignity and their self-esteem. According to the IMF, there were 16 million more unemployed in 2012 than in 2007, most of those in industrialized countries. And that figure is surely an underestimate, since such data is notoriously unreliable.

To staunch the financial hemorrhaging, governments around the world pumped more than $15 trillion into the global economic system, bailing out banks, debt-strapped car companies and insolvent insurance firms. The stated purpose of this Keynesian-style fiscal stimulus: to revive economic growth.

Just a decade earlier, the 1997 Southeast Asian crisis had prefigured the 2008 collapse. The Southeast Asian economy went into freefall in the summer of 1997. In the 18 months prior to the crash more short-term investment had entered the region than in the previous 10 years. Capital flows into Thailand and Malaysia in the 1990s amounted to more than 10 per cent of Gross Domestic Product (GDP) and most of that speculative cash went into short-term debt. Previously, these nations had been more cautious about foreign investment and had taken steps to develop domestic industry by closing the door to cheaper imports from the West.

All that changed in the 1990s when these Southeast Asian countries became star pupils of the so-called 'Washington Consensus'. Both the IMF and the World Bank had advised the countries to deregulate their capital accounts as a way of enticing foreign investment and kick-starting the development process. Around 1990 Thailand, Malaysia, Indonesia and the Philippines all adopted an open-door policy to foreign investment. Measures included jacking up domestic interest rates to attract portfolio investment and pegging the national currency to the dollar to ensure that foreign investors wouldn't get hit in the event of sudden shifts in the value of the currency.

In one of the most thorough examinations of the impact of 'hot money' on national economies, Walden Bello outlines the case of Thailand. In 1994 the World Bank noted in its annual report that 'Thailand provides an excellent example of the dividends to be obtained through outward orientation, receptivity to foreign investment and a market-friendly philosophy backed up by conservative macro-economic management and cautious external borrowing policies.'

Ironically, it was in Thailand that the economic boom first began to fizzle – sparked by the herd mentality of short-term investors. In 1992-93 the country gave in to IMF pressure and adopted a radical deregulation of its financial system.[6] Measures included: fewer constraints on the portfolio management of financial institutions and commercial banks; looser rules on the expansion of banks and financial institutions; dismantling of foreign-exchange controls; and the establishment of the Bangkok International Banking Facility (BIBF). The BIBF was a way for both local and foreign banks to take part in offshore and onshore lending. Firms licensed by the BIBF could both accept deposits and make loans in foreign currencies, to residents and non-residents. Most of the foreign capital entering the country soon came in the form of BIBF dollar loans.

The capital that flooded into Thailand was neither patient nor rooted. Most of it was invested not in goods-producing industries but in areas where profits were reckoned to be sizable and quick. Millions poured into the stock market (which inflated prices beyond their real worth) and into real estate and various kinds of easy consumer credit like car financing. By late 1996 there was an estimated $24 billion in 'hot money' in Bangkok alone. As a result of this offshore investment, the country's foreign debt ballooned from $21 billion in 1988 to $89 billion in 1996. The vast majority of this – more than 80 per cent – was owed to the private sector.[7]

The Asian meltdown

It was a similar story throughout the region. South Korea's foreign debt nearly tripled from $44 billion to $120 billion from 1993 to 1997 – and about 70 per cent of that was in short-term, easily withdrawn funds. In Indonesia, companies outside the financial sector built up $40 billion in debt by the middle of 1997, 87 per cent of which was short-term. According to official figures the five countries in the region (Indonesia, Thailand, Malaysia, the Philippines and South Korea) had a combined debt to foreign banks of $274 billion just before the crisis: 64 per cent of that was in short-term obligations. This was a recipe for financial disaster.

Much of the speculative capital in Thailand went into real estate, always a favorite for those with a get-rich-quick dream in mind. So much money was pumped into Thai real estate that the value of unsold office buildings and apartments in the country nudged $20 billion. It was this massive bubble that finally frayed the nerves of foreign investors. When they woke up to the fact that most of their money was tied up in property, for which there were no buyers, and that Thai banks were carrying billions in bad debt that could not be serviced, investors panicked and hurried to withdraw their funds. The anxiety (later dubbed the 'contagion effect') spread quickly from Thailand and Malaysia to Indonesia, the Philippines and South Korea. Like the plague in medieval Europe, this financial chaos was felt to be a contagious disease that could jump national borders.

In just over a year there was a complete turnaround in the capital account of the region: in 1996, new financial inflows to the five countries totalled $93 billion. In 1997, $105 billion left those same countries – a net outflow of $12 billion. All investors rushed for the exit at the same time because none of them wanted to get caught with depreciated local currency and assets.[8]

The vicious downward spiral picked up speed – egged on by speculators who intervened massively in foreign-exchange markets and helped to seriously devalue local currencies. Under speculative attack, the governments of the region did what they could to ward off the inevitable. The first line of defense was to raid their own foreign-exchange reserves to buy up their national currency in a last-ditch attempt to maintain its value. Under pressure from speculators, the Bank of Thailand lost almost all its $38.7 billion in foreign exchange holdings in just six months. But to no avail. Speculators continued to bail out in droves. The next step was to float their currencies, but that too backfired, proving a catalyst for further devaluation. The Thai *baht* lost half its value in a few months. So the hemorrhage of foreign funds helped both to deplete foreign-exchange reserves and to drive down the value of domestic currencies.

The *baht* felt the pressure first but the devaluation soon spread to the other countries. As the currencies drifted downwards, local firms that had borrowed from abroad had to pay more in local currency for the foreign exchange needed to service their overseas debts. At the first sign that things were spinning out of control, many foreign banks and other creditors refused to roll over their loans. They demanded immediate repayment. At this point the panic that gripped the region suddenly became a crisis threatening to capsize the entire global economy. Soon, international financial operators were selling *baht*, *ringgit* and *rupiah* in an effort to cut potential losses and get their funds safely back to Europe and the US. In the ensuing capital flight, Asian stock prices plunged and the value of local currencies collapsed. Businesses that had taken out dollar-denominated loans couldn't afford the dollar payments to Western creditors.

For a time, governments tried to stave off default by lending some of their foreign-currency reserves to the indebted private companies. South Korea used up some $30 billion in this way. But the money soon ran out and Western banks refused to make new loans or to roll over old debts. Asian businesses defaulted, cutting output and laying off workers. As the region's economies sputtered, panic intensified. Asian currencies lost 35 to 85 per cent of their foreign-exchange value, driving up prices on imported goods and pushing down the standard of living. Businesses large and small were driven to bankruptcy by the sudden drying up of credit; within a year, millions of workers had lost their jobs while the prices of imports, including basic foodstuffs, soared.

In an effort to calm investors and forestall total financial collapse the International Monetary Fund (IMF) introduced a $120-billion bailout plan. But the IMF rescue package just made a bad situation worse – not least for the citizens of those nations who had to endure the impact of the Fund's loan conditions. One of the central requirements of the package was that governments guarantee continued debt service to the private sector in return for creditors being persuaded to roll over or restructure their loans. This mirrored the IMF's role during the Third World debt crisis of the 1980s. Public money from Northern taxpayers (via the

Fund) was handed over to indebted governments, and then recycled to commercial banks in the South to pay off their debts to private investors. In Asia some critics dubbed this bailout of international creditors 'socialism for the global financial elite'.

The IMF's Asian package also forced countries to further liberalize their capital account. The goal was to cut government expenditure and produce a surplus. The standard tools were applied: high interest rates combined

Market buzz

A pocket guide to the language of the financial market place.

• **Hedging**

If a business holds stocks of a commodity like cocoa or copper it runs the risk of losing money if the price falls before it can unload it all. This loss can be avoided by 'hedging' the risk. This involves selling the item before the purchaser actually wants it – ie for delivery at an agreed price at a future date. Hedge funds make a business of selling and buying this risk, often using borrowed money to put together 'highly leveraged' deals. The most infamous hedge fund, the US firm Long Term Capital Management (LTCM), had to be rescued with a $3.5 billion bailout from other Wall Street investment companies after it overextended itself to the tune of $200 billion. The firm had invested $500 million of borrowed money for every $1 million it invested of its own cash.

• **Futures, options and swaps**

A futures contract is an agreement to buy or sell a commodity or shares or currency at a future date at a price decided when the contract is first agreed. An option is like a futures contract except that in this case there is a right, but no obligation, to trade at an agreed price at a future date. An interest-rate swap is a transaction by which financial institutions change the form of their assets or debts. Swaps can be between fixed and floating rate debt, or between debt in different currencies.

• **Derivatives**

A sweeping, catchall term used to refer to a range of extremely complex and obscure financial arrangements. Futures contracts, futures on stock market indices, options and swaps are all derivatives. In general, derivatives are tradable securities whose value is 'derived' (thus the name) from some underlying instrument which may be a stock, bond, commodity or currency. They can be used as a hedge to reduce risks or for speculation.

with cuts to both government expenditures and subsidies to basics like food, fuel and transport. The high interest rates were supposed to be the bait to lure back foreign capital. But the bait didn't work. Tight domestic credit, combined with high interest rates, sparked a much sharper recession than would have otherwise taken place and did nothing to restore investor confidence.

Output in some countries fell 16 per cent or more, unemployment soared and wages nose-dived. In

---

According to the Bank for International Settlements the notional value of all derivatives in effect in June 2007 was $516 trillion, which dwarfs the value of all the world's stock markets combined.

- **Stock market indices**

The most famous are the Dow Jones Industrial Average, an index of share prices on the US stock market based on 30 leading US companies, the FTSE 100, an index of Britain's 100 top companies and the Japanese equivalent, the NIKKEI 225.

- **Foreign exchange market**

This is where currencies are traded. There is no single location for this market since it operates via computer and telephone connections in an interlaced web linking hundreds of trading points all over the world. The total turnover of world foreign exchange markets is enormous, many times the total international trade in goods and services.

- **Mutual funds/Unit trusts**

A financial institution which holds shares on behalf of investors. The investors buy shares or 'units' in the fund, which uses their money to buy shares in a range of companies. An investor selling back the units gets the proceeds of selling a fraction of the fund's total portfolio rather than just shares in one or two companies.

- **Equities**

The ordinary shares or common stock of companies. The owners of these shares are entitled to the residual profits of companies after all claims of creditors, debenture holders and preference shareholders have been satisfied. These are paid out to stock owners in the form of dividends.

- **Junk bonds**

Bonds issued on very doubtful security by firms where there is serious doubt as to whether interest and redemption payments will actually be made. Because these bonds are so risky, lenders are only prepared to hold them if promised returns are high enough.

Thailand, GDP growth-rate estimates plummeted after the IMF intervention, from 2.5 per cent in August 1997 to minus 3.5 per cent in February 1998. In Indonesia, the IMF forced the Government to close down 16 banks; a move it thought would restore confidence in the notoriously inefficient banking system. Instead it led to panic withdrawals by customers at the remaining banks, which brought further chaos. It is estimated that half the businesses in the country went bankrupt.

The impact on the region was stunning. According to the International Labour Organization (ILO) more than 20 million people in Indonesia were laid off from September 1997 to September 1998. UNICEF said that 250,000 clinics were closed. The Asian Development Bank said that more than six million children dropped out of school. And Oxfam estimated that over 100 million Indonesians were living in poverty a year after the crisis – four times more than two years earlier.[9]

There was also a frightening resurgence of racial 'scapegoating' and inter-communal violence throughout the region. Malaysia's leader at the time, the autocratic Mahathir Mohamad, blamed Jewish financiers for destabilizing his Muslim country, while in Indonesia the shops of ethnic-Chinese merchants were looted and burned and hundreds of Chinese brutally beaten and killed.

There were, however, some clear winners that emerged from the Asian meltdown. The big ones were the Western corporate interests that rushed in to snap up the region's bargain-basement assets after the economic collapse. As former US Trade Representative Mickey Kantor said at the time, the recession in the 'Tiger Economies' was a golden chance for the West to reassert its commercial interests. 'When countries seek help from the IMF,' he said, 'Europe and America should use the IMF as a battering ram to gain advantage.'[10]

That was certainly true in South Korea, where the IMF agreement lifted restrictions on outside ownership so that foreigners could purchase up to 55 per cent of Korean companies and 100 per cent of Korean banks. Years of effort by the Korean elite to keep businesses firmly under control of state-supported conglomerates called *chaebols* were undone in a matter of months. In January 1998, the French investment firm Crédit Lyonnais estimated that just 87 of the country's 653 non-financial firms were safe from foreign buyers. US economist Rudi Dornbusch. accurately summed up the overall impact of the economic slump: 'Korea is now owned and operated by our Treasury. That's the positive side of this crisis.'[11]

Why capital controls offer protection

A key reason why the Asian economies were so vulnerable to currency destabilization was that they had gradually abandoned controls over the movement of capital. When a country cedes control over capital flows, it effectively removes any tools it may have for intervening in the market process, leaving itself at the mercy of speculators whose only concern is profit. More critically, nations lose the ability to control internal economic strategies which lie at the heart of national sovereignty. How can a nation hope to determine its own social agenda and economic future if key policy areas are shaped by the self-interest of foreign investors and money markets?

At the time of the Asian meltdown, one country emerged from the chaos in noticeably better shape than the others. Although Malaysia's GDP fell by 7.5 per cent in 1998, the nation managed to escape the devastating social impact felt elsewhere. Partly this was because Malaysia adopted a range of defensive measures to limit capital flight, many of which were modelled on China's example.

The Malaysian Central Bank ruled that private companies could only contract foreign loans if they could show that the loans would end up producing foreign exchange which then could be used to service the debt. And like China, Malaysia also pegged its currency, the *ringgit*, to the US dollar and allowed it to be freely converted to other foreign currencies for trade and direct investment. Critically, portfolio investors had to keep their funds inside Malaysia for a minimum of one year and the amount of money residents could take out of the country was restricted.

Most important, trade in *ringgit* outside the country was not recognized by the government and this helped to prevent manipulation by currency speculators. Measures were also taken to reduce foreign investment in the Malaysian stock market. The controls allowed the government to stimulate the domestic economy with tax cuts, lower interest rates and spending on public infrastructure – without having to worry about speculators targeting its currency. Interest rates fell from 11 to 7 per cent, a helpful boon to local businesses and the domestic banking industry.

Despite its authoritarian political structure, China was also able to sidestep the Asian trap – mainly by avoiding becoming entangled in international financial markets. At the time of the Asian financial crisis, China had considerably more control over its domestic economy than just about any nation in the world. Its currency, the *renminbi*, was not freely convertible; its finance system was owned and controlled by the state and there was relatively little foreign investment in the Chinese stock market. Plus the world's biggest nation was not then a member of the WTO – the country did not become a full member of the organization until December 2001.

As a result, China was not vulnerable to the specu-lative herd behavior that devastated other countries in the region. Instead of devaluing its currency and trying to grab a share of its neighbors' exports, China took another tack. The government decided to direct national savings into a \$200-billion public-works program to stimulate its domestic economy.[12]

Latin American responses

Chile is another country that successfully tried to regulate destabilizing short-term flows of foreign capital by installing a series of financial 'speed bumps' to slow down speculation. When Mexico's economy crashed in 1995, Chile was able to escape the worst 'contagion' effects because of its *encaje* policy. This regulation required foreign investors to deposit funds equivalent to 30 per cent of their investment in Chile's central bank. In addition, portfolio investors were required to keep their cash inside the country for a minimum of at least a year. These barriers slowed down the exodus of funds from Chile and kept it from falling victim to what the financial press dubbed Mexico's 'tequila effect'.

Shaken by the Asian debacle, Western finance ministers, led by the US, came up with a new plan to aid countries experiencing balance-of-payments shortfalls before such a crisis occurred. The idea was to give more money (up to $90 billion) and more power to the IMF to create 'an enhanced IMF facility for countries pursuing strong IMF-approved policies'. The thinking was that an instant loan from a 'precautionary fund' would make currency speculators less anxious and so tame the 'hot money' and stall devaluation.

Brazil was the first country to use the new IMF plan. Unfortunately, Brazil's economy seemed no more immune to financial crisis than Indonesia or Thailand. When the Brazilian *real* came under attack in 1998 the government of Fernando Cardoso spent more than $40 billion in foreign exchange trying to prop it up. Cardoso also raised domestic interest rates to 50 per cent to try to keep capital from fleeing the country. Nevertheless traders continued to hammer the *real* even after the country signed a formal letter of intent with the IMF. By January 1999, nearly a billion dollars a day was exiting the country – the government had no choice but finally to devalue its currency, which lost nearly a third of its value overnight.

The Brazilian economy crashed as IMF policies kicked in. High interest rates scared off domestic business owners who could no longer afford to borrow. Budget cuts and public-sector layoffs increased poverty and unemployment as the government was forced to implement what the IMF called 'the largest privatization program in history'. As in Asia, the IMF/US Treasury plan championed foreign investment, lured by high interest rates, as Brazil's only long-term hope. Unfortunately, the Fund brushed aside the downside of interest-rate hikes – each percentage increase added millions to debt-service costs, all of which had to be repaid in hard currencies purchased with the devalued Brazilian real. By the end of 1999, Brazil's total external debt, always the highest in the Global South, topped more than $230 billion.

The next Latin American nation to feel the pinch was Argentina, one of the first Latin nations fervently to embrace globalization. In December 2001, the country sent shockwaves around the world when the economy exploded into social chaos. In less than two weeks, five different presidents tried to take control and calm the increasingly violent demonstrations which had erupted across the country. '*Que se vayan todos!*' the protesters chanted: 'Out with the lot of them!' – meaning all the politicians and the international financiers that had helped bring the country to its knees.

The crisis had its roots in the economic model pushed by the IMF in the early 1990s when Carlos Menem was President. In return for emergency balance-of-payments support, Argentina knocked down its trade barriers, liberalized its capital account and instituted a massive privatization of state enterprises. Nearly 400 companies – from oil and water to steel, insurance, telephone and postal services – were sold off to foreign interests. Corruption was rife: Menem and his cronies grew rich in the process.

But what really attracted speculators was the

government's move to peg the Argentine peso to the US dollar at an exchange rate of one-to-one. This effectively removed all control over the domestic economy from the hands of the government. The IMF happily endorsed the arrangement.

Then things began to unravel. With a fixed exchange rate and the dollar rising in value, Argentine goods quickly became uncompetitive, both globally and locally. Cheaper imports flooded the country as the once-thriving agricultural sector slumped. Even the world-famous Argentine beef industry saw export markets dry up. The country had to borrow more foreign currency to finance the growing trade gap, further increasing an already heavy debt burden. Soon lenders began to get the jitters, credit disappeared and businesses lurched into bankruptcy.

In December 2001, Argentina again approached the IMF for a loan to meet its $140-billion external debt. When the Fund balked, the country defaulted on $100 billion of its debt, and then quickly spiralled into recession. In a few short months, unemployment spiked to 21 per cent, GDP declined nearly 17 per cent and more than half of Argentineans were living below the poverty line. Something had to give.

Fed up with political corruption and the destructive impact of foreign debt, the Argentine people began to demand more control over their economic lives. The collapse sparked a flurry of worker-run enterprises, co-operatives, alternative currencies, barter exchanges and other self-help institutions. More than 200 companies were taken over and managed by their employees after their owners shut up shop.

In May 2003, the populist government of Nestor Kirchner was elected. In a bold move, Kirchner told debtors he would write off 75 per cent of his country's $100-billion debt in defaulted government bonds – take it or leave it. In September 2003 he also convinced the IMF to roll over $21 billion in outstanding debt, insisting that no more than three per cent of the nation's budget would be used for debt servicing. Pushed to the wall, the IMF caved in.

'We are not going to repeat the history of the past,' said Kirchner. 'For many years we were on our knees before financial organizations and the speculative funds... We've had enough!'[13]

In an astonishing turnaround, the country finally cleared its account with the Fund in January 2006, repaying $9.57 billion in debt and gaining a measure of economic autonomy not felt for decades.

It wasn't easy. Argentina got no help from the IMF along the way. The Fund opposed policies that led to recovery – a stable exchange rate, low interest rates and a tax on exports. A stable currency was important to keep the peso from becoming overvalued. Priced competitively, exports would grow and encourage local investment. Instead the IMF wanted to increase the price of public services like water and electricity, run bigger budget surpluses and pay off foreign creditors, all to please the markets. But the Kirchner government held fast – and the economy responded by growing by nearly nine per cent yearly from 2003 to 2008. Social spending tripled in real terms. Employment rose to a record high and real wages increased by over 40 per cent. Consequently, poverty declined and inequality was reduced.

This was an amazing accomplishment, all the more so because the country continued to service its other debts during that time. By 2005 more than 75 per cent of Argentina's creditors had agreed to debt restructuring and by 2010 more than 90 per cent had reached an agreement.

Not that Argentina is completely out of the woods. Since 2012 the country has been under attack by billionaire hedge fund manager Paul Singer and his company, NML Capital. Singer snapped up millions of dollars' worth of Argentine debt in 2006 for pennies on the dollar and since then has been squeezing the country at every opportunity. NML Capital is looking for a 1,600-per-cent return on its bonds. Singer's 'vulture fund' has even attempted to seize Argentine assets overseas, a claim that was bolstered by Judge Thomas Griesa of the US District Court of New York in the summer of 2014. Griesa ruled that Argentina must pay Singer all the debt claimed before continuing to service the bonds it restructured in 2005 and 2010. (The Court also upheld NML's demand that Argentina identify overseas assets that can be seized in lieu of repayment.) But even servicing its restructured debt has taken a toll. The country has paid more than $174 billion in interest since 2004. Yet total debt has actually increased over that period from $43 billion to more than $240 billion.[14]

Still resisting regulation

Despite the obvious danger of capital ricocheting around the globe, the IMF and the US Treasury have been reluctant to support mechanisms to inhibit its movement. And speculators themselves have also been working overtime to squelch defensive government action against their attacks. Pressures to lift exchange controls were strong right up to the most recent financial 2008 crisis, which is covered in Chapter 7.

The original Bretton Woods agreement did not fulfil Keynes' dream of giving 'every member government the explicit right to control capital movements', but the policies did give members some controls. Unfortunately, even these limited tools have been gradually eroded over the years by the growing insistence on deregulation. Market fundamentalists like Lawrence Summers, formerly Bill Clinton's Treasury Secretary and chief economic advisor to Barack Obama, criticized efforts by Malaysia, Hong Kong and others to hobble the movement of overseas capital.

He called controls a 'catastrophe' and urged countries

to 'open up to foreign financial-service providers, and all the competition, capital and expertise they bring with them'. Given the damage inflicted on millions by the fickle nature of short-term speculators, Summers' views are both myopic and harmful. The fact that he is still a powerful Washington insider does not instil confidence that the radical regulatory changes needed to fend off future economic disasters will be made.

As citizens from Korea to Argentina have seen their lives wrecked by the whipsaw effect of one global financial crisis after another, it has become painfully evident that the old ways no longer work. The world has been led to the brink of financial chaos too often over the last few decades. Solutions are needed urgently to ensure that money markets, bond traders and currency speculators are brought under the control of national governments for the public good.

1 'Global FX volume reaches $5.3 trillion a day in 2013 – BIS', Reuters, 5 Sept 2013 and International Trade World, OECD StatExtracts, stats.oecd.org. **2** Jagdish Bhagwati, 'The Capital Myth: the difference between the trade in widgets and the trade in dollars', *Foreign Affairs*, May/Jun 1998. **3** Walden Bello, *Dilemmas of Domination*, Zed Books, London, 2005. **4** 'Global Currency Trading Volumes Show October Increase', *Wall Street Journal*, 28 Jan 2014, online.wsj.com/articles **5** *IMF Coordinated Portfolio Investment Survey*, cpis.imf.org. **6** Walden Bello, 'Domesticating Markets', *Multinational Monitor*, Mar 1999. **7** Testimony of Walden Bello before the House Banking Committee, US House of Representatives, 21 Apr 1998. **8** *Human Development Report 1999*, UNDP/Oxford University Press. **9** Oxfam East Asia Briefing, available from oxfam.org.uk **10** Quoted in Mark Weisbrot, 'Globalization for Whom?', Preamble Center, preamble.org/globalization **11** Quoted in 'Asian Crisis Spurs Search for New Global Rules', *Economic Justice Report*, Jul 1998. **12** Mark Weisbrot, 'The Case for National Economic Sovereignty', Third World Network Features, Jul 1999. **13** Roger Burbach, 'Can't pay, won't pay', *New Internationalist* No 374, Dec 2004. **14** 'We don't owe, we won't pay!' Jubilee South, Jul 2014, dialogo2000.blogspot.co.uk

6 Poverty, the environment and the market

Faith in economic growth as the key to progress comes into question as the earth's life-support systems fray and signs of ecological collapse multiply. Globalization, geared to spur rapid growth through greater resource consumption, is straining the environment and widening gaps between rich and poor. The standard cure of orthodox market economics – privatization, tax cuts and foreign investment – is not effective. Criticism and concern grows from both expert insiders and grassroots communities.

Whether they are disciples of Keynes, confirmed free-marketeers or top-down central planners, economists of all stripes have an abiding faith in the healing powers of economic growth. Keynesians opt for government regulation and an active fiscal policy to kick-start growth in times of economic malaise. They believe the impact of state spending will catalyze the economy, create jobs and stimulate consumption. Keynesians (and the Left in general) have been concerned with making sure that the growing economic pie was distributed fairly. Socialists and some trade unionists have held out for more control over the production process by workers themselves.

Market fundamentalists, sometimes called 'neo-liberals', hope to boost consumption using different levers. They opt for 'pure' market solutions – tax cuts and low interest rates – both of which are supposed to increase spending and investment by putting more money into people's pockets.

But, until recently, all sides have ignored the environment. The increasingly global economy is completely dependent on the larger economy of the planet. And evidence is all around us that the Earth's ecological health is in severe trouble.

Our system of industrial production has chewed through massive quantities of non-renewable natural resources over the past two centuries. Not only are we wiping out ecosystems and habitats at an alarming rate, but it is also clear that we are exploiting our natural resource base (the economy's 'natural capital') and generating waste at a rate which exceeds the capacity of the natural world to regenerate and heal itself.

We don't have to look far for proof that growth-centered economics is pushing the regenerative capacities of the planet's ecosystems to the brink. There is concern that the supply of oil – the most essential non-renewable resource for the industrialized economy – has already peaked, despite the recent uptick in global supply. The world oil market is subject to booms and busts. But in the long term petroleum is a finite resource. The rate of new discovery has been dwindling for decades.

With other raw materials it is a slightly different story: there is no immediate shortage. Even at current rates of consumption there is enough copper, iron and nickel to last centuries. More pressing is the cumulative impact of relentless resource extraction on the basic life-support systems that we take for granted. The water cycle, the composition of the atmosphere, the assimilation of waste and recycling of nutrients, the pollination of crops, and the delicate interplay of species: all these are threatened.

There is now a large body of research documenting this precipitous decline. Deserts are spreading, forests are hacked down, fertile soils are ruined by erosion and desalination, fisheries are exhausted, species pushed to extinction and groundwater reserves pumped dry. Carbon-dioxide levels in the atmosphere continue to rise due to our extravagant burning of fossil fuels. The Intergovernmental Panel on Climate Change (IPCC) – 2,500 of the world's top climate scientists – says that climate change will lead to 'widespread economic, social and environmental dislocation over the next century'.

Climate-change skeptics may scoff but the scientific consensus is clear. In November 2014 the IPCC released its review of more than 30,000 climate change studies, concluding that emissions from fossil fuels will need to drop to zero by the end of the century to avoid 'irreversible' and damaging impacts on people and the environment.

The International Union for Conservation of Nature (IUCN) stresses that the global extinction crisis is accelerating, with dramatic declines in the populations of many species, including reptiles and primates. The Swiss-based NGO sees habitat loss, human exploitation and invasion by alien species as major threats to wildlife. The loss of habitat is affecting 89 per cent of all threatened birds, 83 per cent of threatened mammals and 91 per cent of threatened plants. The highest number of threatened mammals and birds are found in lowland and mountain tropical rain forests: 900 bird species and 55 per cent of all mammals.

The IUCN concludes we are losing species faster than any time in history – 1,000 to 10,000 times more quickly than the natural rate of extinction that occurs through evolution. Between a third and a half of terrestrial species are expected to die out over the next two centuries if current trends continue unchecked. Scientists reckon the normal extinction rate is one species every four years.[1]

From 1950 to 2014, global economic output jumped from $4.0 trillion to nearly $77.6 trillion – an increase of nearly 2,000 per cent. We have consumed more of the world's natural capital in this brief period than during the entire history of humankind.

Ecological footprints

The ecologists William Rees and Mathis Wackernagel pioneered the 'ecological footprint' concept, which attempts to put a number on the amount of ecological space occupied by people and by nations. They estimate that around 4-6 hectares of land are used to maintain the consumption of the average person in the West. However, the total available productive land in the world is about 1.7 hectares per person (total land divided by population). The difference between the two is what they call 'appropriated carrying capacity' – which basically means the rich are living off the resources of the poor.

The Netherlands, for example, consumes the output of a productive land mass 14 times its size. Most Northern countries and many urban regions in the South already consume more than their fair share; they depend on trade (using someone else's natural assets) or on depleting their own natural capital. According to Rees and Wackernagel, the global footprint now exceeds global biocapacity by 20 per cent and that gap is growing yearly. The US alone, with 4.5 per cent of the world's population, sucks up 25 per cent of the earth's biocapacity. The average Indian has an ecological footprint of just 0.8 hectares while the average American has an ecological footprint of 9.7 hectares.[2]

Regions like North America and western Europe, argue Rees and Wackernagel, 'run an unaccounted ecological deficit – their population either appropriating carrying capacity from elsewhere or from future generations'.[3]

Faith in economic growth as the ultimate hope for human progress is widespread. A central tenet of economists on both left and right has been that the 'carrying capacity' of the Earth is infinitely expandable. The underlying belief is that a combination of ingenuity and technology will eventually allow us all to live like middle-class Americans – if we can only ignore the naysayers and keep the economy growing.

But endless, exponential growth is impossible in a world of finite resources and ecological limits. As the Worldwatch Institute points out: 'Rising demand for energy, food and raw materials by 2.5 billion Chinese and Indians is already having ripple effects worldwide...

Globalization

If China and India were to consume resources and produce pollution at the current US per-capita level, it would require two planet Earths just to sustain their two economies.'[2]

Says ecologist Robert Ayres: 'There is every indication that human economic activity, supported by perverse trade and growth policies, is well on the way to perturbing our natural environment more and faster than any known event in planetary history.'[4]

Ayres is on to something when he accuses the 'perverse' aspects of globalization of accelerating the process of environmental decline. Export-led growth and developing-world debt have combined to speed up the rapid consumption of the Earth's irreplaceable natural resources. Some environmentalists argue that primary resources (nature's goods and services) are too cheap and that their market price does not reflect either their finite nature or the hidden social and ecological costs of extraction. Instead, they suggest, we should conserve the resources we have by making them more expensive. There is some truth to this analysis. The price of raw materials is notoriously unpredictable, based not just on supply and demand but also on the monopoly power of corporations that control distribution and sales. In general, when the global economy booms, overall demand goes up. When the economy crashes, as it did in 2008, demand falls. In recent years, the price of industrial metals like nickel, copper and iron has risen (or fallen) in tandem with the Chinese economy, the engine of global production at the moment. World market prices for commodities like cotton, sugar and coffee also gyrate unpredictably. Prior to the 2008 global meltdown, world energy prices nearly tripled and commodity prices across the board rose sharply, including the prices of staples like corn and rice.

This instability has been compounded in recent years by the 'financialization' of commodity trading, the latest twist of the 'casino economy' (see Chapter 5). Big banks, hedge funds and money managers scour the globe for opportunities to invest surplus capital to reap the biggest returns in the shortest time. The lessons of the 2008 crash, it seems, have yet to be learned. Short-term financial flows continue to unsettle the world economy. In the year 2000, commodity assets controlled by finance capital amounted to $10 billion; by 2012 that figure had topped $439 billion. UNCTAD notes that short-term investors twist commodity markets so that 'prices are detached from supply and demand'. This leads to 'high volatility and distorted prices' – generating tidy profits for speculators but financial insecurity for farmers, miners and nations whose income depends on these markets.[5]

Humanity's footprint

The world's demand is outstripping the earth's biocapacity so we are beginning to consume irreplaceable natural capital. The average ecological footprint worldwide is 2.6 hectares while the average biocapacity available per person is 1.7 hectares. Humanity's footprint now exceeds the planet's regenerative capacity by 50%. Our footprint has more than doubled since 1961.

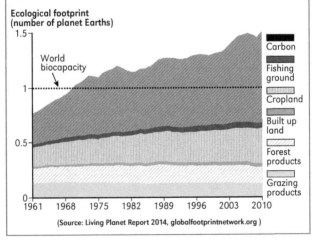

Ecological footprint (number of planet Earths)

World biocapacity

Carbon
Fishing ground
Cropland
Built up land
Forest products
Grazing products

(Source: Living Planet Report 2014, globalfootprintnetwork.org)

But debt in developing countries, the source of many of the world's commodities, has also kept prices low. Centuries of colonialism put in place a system of extreme dependency on a narrow range of exports which remains to this day. According to UNCTAD, just three commodities account for 75 per cent of total exports in each of the 48 poorest nations. This might be tolerable if nations like Honduras, Kenya and Zambia earned a decent income from their sugar, tea and copper. Sadly, the opposite is true. Due to plunging 'terms of trade', commodity-dependent nations need to export more just to stay in the same place. Even when times are good, things are bad. Take the 2002-12 'commodity supercycle' when the world's voracious appetite for raw materials and new energy resources drove up commodity prices. Export income increased. But so did dependency. UNCTAD notes that 57 per cent of developing countries now depend on resources for at least 60 per cent of their export earnings.[5] The UN agency's figures show a long-running deterioration in the prices of primary commodities vis-à-vis manufactures.

A mountain of debt doesn't help. The price of admission to the global trading community means that poor countries are obliged to service their debts before they are allowed to do anything else. They are urged to expand commodity exports to world markets by hook or by crook. Unfortunately, removing the barriers to exports isn't always the answer. In fact, it can make matters worse, especially for small farmers. When they grow more for export, it often leads, perversely, to overproduction and lower prices. Faced with less income, farmers respond rationally by increasing their production, ensuring that prices remain low. Countries in hock have been forced by World Bank and IMF structural adjustment edicts to ratchet up exports to service their debts. The new term circulating among critical economists to describe the phenomenon is 'immiserating trade'. The more you trade, the poorer you get.[6]

How boosting exports can backfire

Globalization's default position is market efficiency. But this often plays into the hands of those who can 'game' the system. If all poor countries have to increase their exports at once, there is a glut and prices fall – sometimes by half. Twice as much has to be exported to earn the same amount of foreign currency. The winners are the developed countries and Western-based corporations. They not only get their debts serviced, but they also benefit from cheap resources which helps keep prices down, profits up and inflation under control in the North. The losers are the people of the South (especially those without oil) and the global environment.

Globalization puts the squeeze on the environment by turbo-charging the extractive industries. Take Brazil, which environmentalists consider one of the earth's most ecologically important nations. The country still contains 30 per cent of the planet's rainforest; the sprawling Amazon region has long been considered 'the lungs of the world'. Scientists believe the spectacular biological diversity of the rainforest is a potential cornucopia of priceless, life-saving drugs.

In 1999, the Brazilian government slashed millions of dollars off environmental spending in the wake of IMF-enforced cuts. The country's environmental enforcement arm had its budget pared by 19 per cent. The Fund's policies then sparked a domestic recession that boosted unemployment, forcing many ordinary workers and peasants to clear larger areas of jungle for subsistence.

Encouraging primary exports can also strengthen the hand of agribusiness and large landowners. Peasant farmers and smallholders are squeezed out by the implacable logic of economic efficiency. In Brazil, the amount of land devoted to large-scale soy production has jumped from 0.2 million hectares to more than 58 million hectares over the past 35 years, much of it virgin rainforest. In 2014, the country harvested 90 million tons of soybeans, replacing the US as the leading soy-producing nation. The growth of the country's beef industry has caused even more environmental destruction in the Amazon. Deforestation rates have dropped dramatically since 2004 when 27,000 square kilometers of rainforest was burned, the second highest rate on record, but still, over the past 40 years, about a fifth of Brazil's jungle has been razed. The vast nation is now the world's biggest beef exporter but the industry's continued expansion threatens 40 per cent of the world's remaining rainforest.[7] In 2013, nearly 6,000 square kilometers of rainforest was cleared. About three-quarters of Brazil's greenhouse gas emissions come from torching the jungle and the country is now the world's sixth-largest carbon-dioxide polluter.[8]

Dr Gustavo Fonseca of the *Universidade Federal de Minas Gerais* in Brazil sums up the concern of environmentalists: 'Our biggest worry now is that the government is going to lose control of attempts to control deforestation. This is undermining the very basis of what we've been trying to accomplish in Brazil.'[9]

The pattern is repeated in neighboring Argentina, where the area planted with soy has tripled in the last decade. Argentina became the first Latin American nation to allow genetically modified soy in 1996. The versatile legume now covers half the country's cultivated land and Argentina is the world's number one exporter of soy, supplying 45 per cent of the world market. The country's 2007 'Forest Law' prohibits clearing forest to plant soy. Yet, according to the UN Food and Agriculture Organisation (FAO), native forests are disappearing at the rate of 240,000 hectares a year. Since 1990, Argentina's forest cover has shrunk by 10 per cent.

Asia's 'economic miracle' has also been built on a fast-track liquidation of its natural resources. In Cambodia, Thailand, Laos, the Philippines and elsewhere, pristine rainforests have been razed, rivers fouled, coastal areas poisoned with pesticides and fisheries exhausted. In the Indonesian capital, Jakarta, more than 70 per cent of water samples were found to be 'highly contaminated by chemical pollutants' while the country's forests were being hacked down at the rate of 2.4 million hectares per year. In the Malaysian state of Sarawak (part of the island of Borneo) 30 per cent of the forest disappeared in a mere two decades, while in peninsular Malaysia 73 per cent of 116 rivers surveyed by authorities were found to be either 'biologically dead' or 'dying'.[10]

The environmental group Friends of the Earth (FoE) summarized the impact of free-market deregulation on Third World environments in its 1999 study, *IMF: Selling the Environment Short*. FoE examined IMF policies in eight countries, including Cameroon, Côte d'Ivoire, Guyana, Nicaragua and Thailand, and found significant negative environmental impacts in all of them.

Several countries slashed government spending after being pressured by the Fund to eliminate budget deficits. The report also noted that IMF policies encourage, and sometimes induce, countries to exploit natural resources at unsustainable rates. According to Carol Welch, co-author of the report: 'Every case shows that the IMF pushes short-term profit at the expense of biodiversity and ecological prosperity... the IMF is undermining people's lives by disregarding environmental issues.'[11]

Persistent poverty has also spurred environmental decline – the poor do not make good eco-citizens. Animals are poached and slaughtered by desperate African villagers for their valuable ivory, their body parts or simply for 'bush meat'.

Madagascar, the huge island nation off the coast of Mozambique, was once covered in lush forests. It has turned into a barren wasteland as people slash and burn jungle plots to grow food. Soil erosion is so serious that the sea around the island sometimes appears blood red from the iron-tinged run-off. The Indian Ocean nation is home to some 200,000 plant and animal species – three-quarters of which are found nowhere else. Less than a tenth of Madagascar is still tree-covered and the forest is vanishing at the rate of 200,000 hectares a year. Illegal logging of costly tropical hardwoods like rosewood and ebony is rampant. One 150-kilogram log of rosewood can fetch as much as $1,300. Poverty is the core of the problem: 70 per cent of the island's 14 million people live on less than a dollar a day. So five dollars a day to work as a logger in the jungle is a lifesaver for impoverished peasants.[12]

'Our village has been burning forests to plant rice here for generations,' Dimanche Dimasy, chief elder of Mahatsara village, told the BBC. 'This is our way of life. If we can't cut the forests, we can't feed ourselves. The government wants to protect the forests but nobody cares about protecting the peasants who live here.'[13]

Taking to the streets in protest

The gospel of globalization is seductive because it is based on a simple principle: free the market of constraints and its creative power will bring employment, wealth and prosperity. But not everyone shares the same faith.

The signs are inescapable – not least of which are the thousands of civil-society groups around the world that have taken their case to the streets. It began in Seattle in November 1999 when more than 50,000 people from dozens of countries demonstrated at the annual meeting of the World Trade Organization. The gathering was a unique mix of environmentalists, trade unionists, peasant organizations, students and ordinary citizens – all united by their concern that economic globalization is spinning out of control. The protest gained worldwide prominence when police in riot gear charged the crowds, firing pepper spray, teargas and plastic bullets. Some 500 people were arrested and a state of emergency was declared.

Then, at the Washington meetings of the IMF and World Bank in April 2000, another 15,000 people gathered for a repeat protest. Ironically, as if to underline the demonstrators' concerns, stock markets nosedived the same week, as a wave of panic selling swept the globe, puncturing the high-tech stock bubble that had carried markets to dizzying new heights through the 1990s. After Seattle, civil-society demonstrations became a regular occurrence at meetings of the IMF/World Bank, the G8 and the expanded G20 – Prague in October 2000, Quebec City in April 2001, Miami in November 2003, Scotland in July 2005, Italy in July 2009, Toronto in June 2010, and Brisbane in November 2014. Wherever these political elites meet, they now run into a similar phalanx of protesters.

Even among mainstream economists globalization is coming under increasing scrutiny. The financial crises in Russia, Asia and Latin America in the late 1990s proved to be a warm-up for the spectacular global crash of 2008. Together these mishaps opened a deep rift in the dominant 'Washington Consensus' – a view that had been promoted by the Bretton Woods institutions and adopted by most Western governments. After 2008, powerful supporters of free trade and open markets began to reconsider their position.

The influential economist Jeffrey Sachs was one of those. Now director of the Earth Institute at Columbia University and special advisor to UN Secretary-General Ban Ki-moon, Sachs was an IMF advisor and one of the main engineers of capitalist 'shock therapy' in Russia after the fall of the Soviet Union. The Asian financial crisis forced him to re-examine his faith in the supremacy of deregulated markets and to question the conventional solutions to national financial crises – especially the role of the IMF. In a candid *Financial Times* article published in December 1997, Sachs called the IMF 'secretive' and 'unaccountable'. 'It defies logic,' he continued, that 'a small group of 1,000 economists on 19th Street in Washington should dictate the economic conditions of life to 75 developing countries with around 1.4 billion people.'

Others began to speak out too. The World Bank's former chief economist, Joseph Stiglitz, became a much-quoted 'ex-insider' willing to criticize publicly the dangerous policies of market fundamentalists.

Globalization and its Discontents, his scathing 2002 critique of the Bretton Woods institutions, became a bestseller, studded with personal anecdotes and case studies.

'The net effect of the policies set by the Washington consensus,' he wrote, 'has all too often been to benefit the few at the expense of the many, the well-off at the expense of the poor. In many cases commercial interests and values have superseded concern for the environment, democracy, human rights, and social justice.'[14]

Stiglitz continues to hammer away at the lunacy of deregulated markets. In September 2014 he wrote in Britain's *Guardian* newspaper: 'What we have been observing – wage stagnation and rising inequality, even as wealth increases – does not reflect the workings of a normal market economy, but of what I call ersatz capitalism. The problem may not be with how markets should or do work, but with our political system, which has failed to ensure that markets are competitive, and has designed rules that sustain distorted markets in which corporations and the rich can (and unfortunately do) exploit everyone else.'[15]

The influential financial journalist Martin Wolf was another globalization propagandist who changed his mind in the light of the global crash. His 2004 book, *Why Globalization Works*, was a song of praise to unrestricted markets. Ten years later, in *Shifts and Shocks*, he recants his earlier enthusiasm, admitting that 'the interaction between liberalism and globalization has destabilized the financial system... To pretend one can return to the intellectual and policy-making status quo is profoundly mistaken.'[16]

Despite the spectacular economic growth of the past half-century, the quality of life for a fifth of the world's population has actually regressed in relative, and sometimes absolute, terms. One of the most cogent critiques of globalization comes from the UN Development Programme. Its yearly *Human Development Report* is a first-rate compilation of insightful data and probing analysis. The prose may be stiff but it gets to the point. 'When the market goes too far in dominating social and political outcomes, the opportunities and rewards of globalization spread unequally and inequitably – concentrating power and wealth in a select group of people, nations and corporations, marginalizing the others.'[17]

The UN agency supports its analysis with telling data on what it calls a 'grotesque and dangerous polarization' between those people and countries benefiting from the system and those that are merely 'passive recipients' of its effects.

Globalization is a false god for the majority of the world's citizens. As Stiglitz points out: 'Despite repeated promises of poverty reduction made over the last decade of the 20th century, the actual number of people living in poverty has actually increased by 100 million.'[14]

Spiralling inequality

The divide is becoming so extreme that more astute members of the business community are beginning to worry. The *Global Wealth Report 2014* from the giant financial services company, Credit Suisse, found that the richest one per cent of the world's population owned 48 per cent of global wealth while the bottom half owned less than one per cent. The world's 500 richest people are a cosmopolitan bunch – they hail from Mexico, Russia, India, China, Britain, the US and elsewhere. And, according to UNDP, they now have a combined income greater than the poorest 416 million of their fellow global citizens.

The OECD, too, has pointed to the enormous increase in income inequality as 'one of the most significant

– and worrying – features of the development of the world economy in the past 200 years.'[18] In 2014, the agency noted that the income of the top 10 per cent of the population in OECD member states is 9.5 times that of the bottom 10 per cent – an increase of more than 30 per cent in 25 years. 'And worryingly for our future,' stressed the OECD's secretary-general, José Ángel Gurría, 'youth have now replaced the elderly as the group experiencing the greatest risk of income poverty.'

The change in income inequality in the rest of the world is checkered, increasing in some countries and decreasing in others. In the most populated developing countries – India, China and Indonesia – equality rose from 1994 to 2013. In most of Latin America, parts of sub-Saharan Africa and Southeast Asia, equality declined slightly. The big success story is Brazil, where inequality fell dramatically as a result of targeted anti-poverty policies. Nonetheless, the wealth gap in Brazil is still amongst the highest in the world. And as UNDP points out: 'the majority of the world's population is still living in countries with stable or increasing inequality, because, in populous countries like India and China, inequality is rising.' China had 250,000 dollar-millionaires in 2005; they made up less than 0.4 per cent of the country's population but held 70 per cent of the country's wealth.[19]

The growing gap can mean the difference between life and death: children born into the poorest 20 per cent of households in Ghana or Senegal are two to three times more likely to die before the age of five than children born into the richest 20 per cent of households.[20] The same holds true in rich countries. A 2014 Statistics Canada study found that income inequality is associated with the premature deaths of 40,000 Canadians a year. Poor males have a 63-per-cent greater chance of dying from heart disease than their wealthy counterparts while poor women have a 160-per-cent greater chance of dying from diabetes.[21]

Wealth is highly concentrated in the hands of relatively few rich people and they're getting richer. In many Western countries the middle class is shrinking and people are actually earning less in real terms (adjusted for inflation) than they were in the 1970s. In Britain, for example, the wealthiest 1 per cent owns the same amount as the bottom 55 per cent and there were 104 billionaires in 2014 – more than triple the number of a decade ago. (London has more billionaires – 72 – than any other city in the world.)

Another UN study concluded that in the 1980s real wages (adjusted for inflation) had fallen and income inequality increased in all OECD countries except Germany and Italy.

In the US, the top one per cent boosted their wealth from 25 per cent of the total in 1973 to 40 per cent in 2014. But the top 0.1 per cent gained even more: in 2013 the top 25 hedge fund managers in the US pocketed, on average, $1 billion each.[22]

This shift in wealth and income from bottom to top is part of the logic of globalization. In order to be 'competitive', governments adopt policies which cut taxes and favor profits over wages. The economic argument is simple: putting more money into the pockets of corporations and wealthy individuals (who benefit most from tax cuts: the higher the income, the greater the gain) is supposed to lead to greater investment, jobs, economic growth and prosperity. Both corporate and individual tax rates have dropped across the industrialized world over the past 35 years. In the US, the top marginal tax rate on wealthy individuals averaged 82 per cent from 1947 to 1974. Then, under President Reagan, the rate was slashed to 28 per cent; in recent years it has hovered around 35 per cent. The UK has followed suit. The Tory/LibDem coalition government of 2010-15 reduced the top rate of tax to 45 per cent while cutting benefits to the poor. Other countries have been less generous to the rich. The top tax rate in Switzerland and

Germany has been stable for 50 years and the top one per cent actually take slightly less of total income than they did in the 1960s.[23]

Unfortunately, there is no evidence that the public is better off as a result of tax cuts for the rich. If the reverse were true, and tax cuts were directed towards people at the bottom of the income ladder, it could make a difference. The money would almost certainly be spent on basic necessities rather than luxury goods. But this isn't part of the globalization game plan. To sum up: in every country that has taken up the 'reduce-taxes-cut--the-deficit' mantra, tax cuts mostly benefit wealthy individuals and corporations. What happens to the extra cash is predictable: some goes into high-priced consumer baubles – a phenomenon which is glaringly visible amongst the elite in cities from Bangkok to Los Angeles. The rest winds up in the stock market, in pricey real estate or in other sorts of non-productive speculation.

Major players are no longer satisfied with modest profits on long-term investment, especially when double-digit returns are available from currency speculation or financial derivatives. This diversion of capital away from socially useful investment fuels the 'casino economy'. That and the fact that investment opportunities in the goods-producing sector are shrinking due to the problem of 'over-capacity' – too many goods chasing too few buyers (see Chapter 5). Computerized robots and automated assembly lines replace workers with new technology, leaving fewer people who can buy the products that factories are churning out. Those that remain find their wages under constant downward pressure in the face of cheaper labor elsewhere. The drive to be competitive ends up being a 'race to the bottom'. Workers who don't lose their jobs find their wages squeezed.

Since the 1980s wages have risen less quickly than productivity, which means that workers are receiving a shrinking share of economic growth. According to the ILO, average real pay in developed economies rose just

0.1 per cent in 2012 and 0.2 per cent in 2013. Workers in Italy, Japan and the UK were earning less than in 2007. Wages used to make up 70 per cent of GDP in the US; that number is now closer to 64 per cent. The same trend is evident even in Scandinavia, according to the OECD. In Norway, labor's share tumbled from 64 per cent in 1980

Mind the gap

Despite decades of increasing per-capita income, and phenomenal growth in China and India, poverty is still an urgent global problem.
- The richest 10% of the world's population receive 42% of world income while the poorest 10% receive just 1%.
- 1.2 billion people live on less than $1.25 a day while 2.7 billion – about 37% of the world's population – live on less than $2.50 a day.
- The world's richest 80 people own the same amount of wealth as the poorest half of the world's population, 3.5 billion people.
- In 2010, high-income countries with 16% of the world's population took home 55% of total income. Low-income countries with 72% per cent of global population earned just 1%.
- The per-capita income gap between high income and low income countries increased from $18,525 in 1980 to $32,900 in 2007, before falling to $32,000 in 2010. Per capita incomes between low and middle income countries more than doubled from around $3,000 in 1980 to $7,600 in 2010.

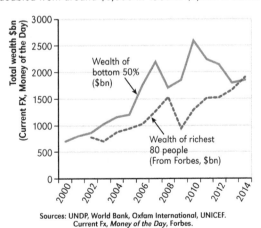

Sources: UNDP, World Bank, Oxfam International, UNICEF.
Current Fx, *Money of the Day*, Forbes.

to 55 per cent in 2013. In Sweden the drop was from 74 per cent to 65 per cent. A decline has also occurred in many developing countries, notably China and Mexico. As the business magazine, *The Economist*, notes: 'The scale and breadth of this squeeze are striking. And the consequences are ugly. Since capital tends to be owned by richer households, a rising share of national income going to capital worsens inequality. In countries where the gap in wages between high earners and the rest has also increased, the two effects compound each other.'[24]

Despite these worrying warning signs, staunch free marketeers are reluctant to abandon their beliefs: 'Give the private sector the resources,' they say, 'it will do the job.' But the proof is elusive. Surplus capital that doesn't get funnelled into the currency markets zips straight into overseas tax havens, where both rich individuals and globe-trotting transnationals have been squirrelling away their cash for decades.

The tyranny of tax havens and the super-rich

There are nearly 70 tax havens scattered around the world. These 'offshore financial centers' include places like the Bahamas, the Cayman Islands, Monaco, Luxembourg and Bermuda. Investors can store their wealth secretly, no questions asked – thus escaping any social obligations to the country where they may have earned it. Only a small number of these tax havens have public disclosure laws affecting the banks which operate within their borders.

A mere fraction of the global population actually lives in tax havens. Yet these enclaves produce about three per cent of world GDP, account for 26 per cent of global financial assets and more than 30 per cent of the profits of US transnationals. This final figure gives a clear sense of how important tax havens are to the corporate world – and why they need to be closed. But it also underlines the flawed reasoning of those who support economic policies premised on tax cuts and corporate deregulation.

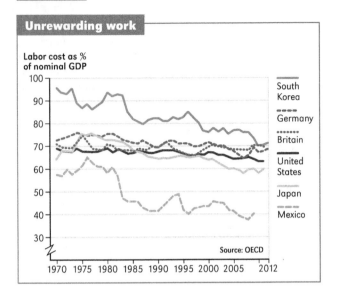

Unrewarding work

Labor cost as %
of nominal GDP

South Korea

Germany

Britain

United States

Japan

Mexico

Source: OECD

1970 1975 1980 1985 1990 1995 2000 2005 2012

In almost all cases, corporations will do whatever they can to avoid paying taxes in order to maximize returns on the investment of their stockholders. That's the way the system works. They jeopardize their own survival to the extent that they are unable to reach that goal.

The tension between the corporate goal of avoiding taxes and the broader public interest is one reason why tax havens are now coming under intense scrutiny. Both OECD and EU members have long recognized these refuges as a drain on national treasuries and a convenient way of 'laundering' illegal funds. For example, the disgraced US energy trading company, Enron, is said to have used 800 different 'financial dumps' in the Caribbean to hide its debts. And it is estimated that up to $500 billion from the global narcotics trade passes through tax havens annually. According to the advocacy group, Canadians for Tax Fairness, Canadians had $170 billion invested in the top 10 tax havens at the end of 2013, up 10 per cent from the previous year and a whopping 188-per-cent jump since 2005. The fear is that digital commerce, combined with lax controls on the free movement of capital, will trigger an even greater flow of wealth and profits to these tax-free enclaves.[25]

The wealth of the super-rich balloons even as the social fabric that forms the backdrop to our lives continues to fray. This is the hidden human cost of 'market discipline' and it is as much a dilemma for social democracies in Europe as it is for politically fragile countries in Africa or Latin America.

In the industrialized nations we can chronicle the gradual decline in public services and social provision that has accompanied attempts to reduce government deficits. This cut-back on public spending is demanded by international markets – by the same investors that demand high rates of return on their investment and low rates of taxation. As corporate profits boom and real wages stagnate, the glue that holds us together is losing its bond. Government revenues are directed to paying down debt or cutting taxes while citizens are told there is no longer enough money to pay for 'public goods'. Middle-class taxpayers may even receive a few hundred dollars in tax savings. But there is a price to be paid. Investment in public infrastructure dwindles and our 'commonwealth' is diminished – there is less money for public education, budgets for parks and recreation are slashed, public transport and state-funded healthcare are underfunded.

In the Western nations, education and healthcare systems have seen repeated budget cuts as the state retreats and makes way for private, profit-oriented ventures. Welfare and unemployment benefits have been 'rationalized', slashing the number of those eligible. Fees for college and university have skyrocketed. In the US, for example, tuition rates have jumped by more than 1,000 per cent since the 1970s and student debt is now approaching $1.2 trillion. (State funding of universities declined by about 40 per cent during that period.)

Meanwhile, senior citizens and those nearing retirement are fearful that promised pensions will evaporate as governments become more desperate for funds. Individuals are frantically scraping together their savings, told by business-friendly politicians that they should look to the stock market as the ticket to old-age security. Tapping into the politics of resentment, some governments are attempting to claw back the hard-won gains of public-sector workers in an attempt to bring everyone down to the same low level of pensions or benefits. Government funding for the arts and for environmental protection has also been steadily eroded. The failure to protect these 'public goods' diminishes us all, makes us less capable of caring for each other and prohibits us from advancing together as a cohesive, mutually supportive community.

How globalization can derail development

Globalization has also derailed development in the Global South, where the poor continue to pay the highest price of adjustment. To boost exports and maintain their obligations to creditors, developing countries divert money away from social spending and infrastructure. There have been countless studies detailing the social impact of economic globalization and the results are depressingly similar. In most of the world's poorest countries, poverty reduction stalled between 1995 and 2005 as they fell further behind richer nations. The most recent global recession will only worsen this trend.

As the Ebola virus raged through West Africa in 2014 a report from three leading British universities concluded that IMF policies favoring international debt repayment over social spending weakened healthcare in the three worst-hit countries. Researchers in *The Lancet* charged that harsh loan conditions imposed on Sierra Leone, Liberia and Guinea led to 'underfunded, insufficiently staffed, and poorly prepared health systems' – a key reason the disease spread so rapidly.[26]

The Indian government launched its campaign to liberalize the economy and open up to foreign investors in 1992. Nearly 25 years later, the giant nation has been transformed. Transnational brands are ubiquitous while sleek German and Japanese cars jostle bullock carts in the streets of Mumbai and Bangalore. High-tech exports are booming, growing at a rate of 12-14 per cent a year. The value of those exports hit $85 billion in 2014. Meanwhile, the country is graduating millions of skilled professionals and foreign capital is pouring in. Microsoft, Intel and Cisco have all announced investments of billions. Rapid growth from 2002-12 lifted tens of millions of Indians from poverty into a middle class that now approaches 300 million in a population of 1.3 billion.

Nonetheless, disparities within the country are widening. Many Indian citizens have seen their living standards fall or stagnate since embracing globalization. India is home to a third of the world's poorest people. A recent study by the McKinsey Global Institute estimates that 56 per cent of Indians, around 680 million, lack the means to meet their basic needs. Most of those are in the rural areas. Another 413 million are considered vulnerable. 'They have only a tenuous grip on a better standard of living, and shocks such as illness or a lost job can easily push them back into desperate circumstances,' the report notes.[27] Malnutrition affects nearly half the country's children and 10 per cent of all boys and a quarter of all girls don't attend primary school, while the death rate for girls age 1-5 is 50 per cent greater than for boys.

Demonstrations continue to erupt across the country as Indians worry about cheap food imports wiping out local farmers. Two influential coalitions uniting hundreds of grassroots organizations are spearheading the protests. The National Alliance of People's Movements is made up of more than 200 citizens' groups and was formed in 1992. The Joint Action Forum of Indian People (JAFIP) against globalization brought together more than 50 farmers' and peasant groups in 1998 to demand that India withdraw from the WTO.

The litany of suffering and damage spawned by harsh market reforms is repeated across the developing world.

A massive study involving hundreds of civil-society groups across eight countries confirms this judgment. The Structural Adjustment Participatory Review Initiative (SAPRI) held hearings from Bangladesh to El Salvador gathering grassroots information over a four-year period, originally with the participation of ex-World Bank President James Wolfensohn. However, the Bank backed out of the process when it realized what would appear in the final report. No wonder. Eventually released in 2001, at the tail end of the Bank's structural-adjustment binge, the SAPRI review confirmed what Northern NGOs and ordinary people in the South had been saying for years: 'Adjustment policies contributed to further impoverishment and marginalization of local populations' while increasing economic inequality.'[28]

In Hungary, the IMF advised introducing liberalized trade, a tight money supply and rapid privatization of state assets. But the report found the policies deflected money away from education and social services and into the wallets of wealthy bond holders.

In Senegal, which had endured 20 years of IMF programs, the report found 'declining quality in education and health' combined with a growth in 'maternal mortality, unemployment and child labor'. In Tanzania, globalization had successfully redirected agriculture towards exports but had also 'expanded rural poverty, income inequality and environmental degradation'. Food security decreased, housing conditions deteriorated and primary-school enrolment dropped, while malnutrition and infant mortality rose.

Meanwhile, millions of Mexican farmers were pushed out of agriculture and thousands of small businesses went bankrupt after the country signed the North American Free Trade Agreement (NAFTA) in 1994. Thanks to

NAFTA, the US was able to dump highly subsidized, cheap maize into Mexico, driving local farmers out of business. In 1990, Mexico was self-sufficient in maize, a crop with deep cultural significance for the Mexican people. Today it's the world's third-largest importer. Two decades after NAFTA, poverty, rural unemployment and overall inequality have increased. The country's economic growth has stalled, averaging less than one per cent since 2000. And Mexico's poverty rate has not budged: at 52 per cent it is identical to 1994. Things would have been much worse if thousands of Mexicans hadn't migrated north in desperation, looking for work.

In all countries touched by economic globalization, women tend to bear a disproportionate share of the costs. One feminist critique of structural adjustment documented many ways in which women become 'shock absorbers' for economic reforms. These include: forcing more women into informal-sector jobs as mainstream opportunities fade; promoting export crops which men tend to dominate; disrupting girls' education; increasing mortality rates and worsening female health; more domestic violence and stress; and an overall increase in the workload of women both inside and outside the home.[29]

Since women are the caregivers in most societies, they tend to pick up the pieces when the social safety net is slashed. A 1997 Zimbabwe study found that 15 years of economic reform had a devastating impact on women in that southern African country. When school fees were raised, girls dropped out first. And when health spending was cut by a third, the number of women dying in childbirth doubled. As male breadwinners are laid off, women do what they can to compensate for the lost income. They brew beer, turn to prostitution or become street traders. It inevitably falls on women to pick up the slack when governments cut education, healthcare and other social programs. In Western countries, too, women bear the brunt of austerity-led spending cuts.

After the 2008 recession the US state of Washington cut $10 billion from its budget. Over half the job cuts were in education, health, and social services where women made up 72 per cent of the labour force.[30]

Are the social and environmental costs of economic growth too great? As the victims of globalization multiply, growing legions of ordinary people are beginning to question a process over which they have no control and little say. It's easy to be a cheerleader for globalization if you're on the winning side. But not so easy if your job has been outsourced to Mexico or China, or your coffee crop no longer brings in enough cash to feed and clothe your family. As the grip of the global economy tightens, millions of ordinary people around the world have begun to speak out forcefully against a system which they see as both harmful and unjust.

Instead of a homogenized global culture shaped by the narrow demands of the 'money economy', there is a resurgent push for equity and sustainability. Instead of a deregulated globalization which rides roughshod over the rights of nation-states and communities, civil-society groups from Bolivia to China are calling for a radical restructuring. The aim is for an economic system more connected to real human needs and aspirations – and less geared to the anti-human machinations of the corporate-led free market. In the next chapter we'll look at how we might get there.

1 millenniumassessment.org/en/index.aspx. **2** C Flavin and G Gardner, 'China, India and the New World Order', *State of the World 2006*, WW Norton, New York, 2006. **3** M Wackernagel & W Rees, *Our Ecological Footprint*, New Society Publishers, 1996. **4** Quoted in Kalle Lasn, 'The global economy is a doomsday machine', see nin.tl/globaldoomsday **5** 'Commodities and Development Report 2012', UNCTAD. **6** Gerald Greenfield, 'Free market freefall', *Focus on the Global South*, focusweb. org **7** George Monbiot, 'The price of cheap beef', *Guardian*, 18 Oct 2005. **8** Damian Carrington, 'Amazon deforestation increased by one-third in past year', *Guardian*, 15 Nov 2013. **9** Anthony Faiola, 'Brazil's sick economy infects the ecosystem', *Guardian Weekly*, 25 Apr 1999. **10** Walden Bello, 'The end of the miracle', *Multinational Monitor*, Jan/Feb 1998. **11** Friends of the Earth, *The IMF: selling the environment short*, see foe.org/res/pubs/pdf/imf.pdf **12** David Braun, 'Madagascar's logging crisis', *National Geographic*, 20 May 2010, nin.tl/madagascarlogging **13** Tim Cocks, 'Malagasy Wilderness in the Balance', BBC news, 14 Feb 2005, nin.tl/malagasywild **14** Joseph Stiglitz, *Globalization and its Discontents*, WW Norton, New York, 2002. **15** 'Capitalism needs new rules ', Joseph Stiglitz, *Guardian*, 2 Sept 2014. **16** Martin Wolf, *The Shifts and Shocks,* Penguin, London, 2014. **17** *Human Development Report 1999*, UNDP, New York, 1999. **18** *How was life? Global well-being since 1820*, OECD, Oct 2014. **19** Martin Hart-Landsberg, 'The US economy and China', *Monthly Review*, Feb 2010. **20** *Human Development Report 2005*, UNDP, New York, 2005. **21** D Raphael & T Bryant, 'Income inequality is a deadly problem', *Toronto Star*, 24 Nov 2014. **22** Paul Krugman, 'The Rich but invisible', *New York Times*, Oct 4/5 2014. **23** Danny Dorling, 'How the super rich got richer: 10 shocking facts about inequality', *Guardian*, 15 Sep 2014. **24** 'Pay and economic growth', *Economist,* 2 Nov 2013. **25** Madelaine Drohan, 'No mean feat to crack down on tax havens', *Globe and Mail*, Toronto, 12 Apr 2000. **26** Michelle Faul, 'Ebola crisis made worse by IMF austerity plans for Africa', AP, 30 Dec 2014. **27** Richard Dobbs & Anu Madgavkar, 'Five myths about India's poverty', *Huffington Post*, 2 Jun 2014. **28** 'The policy roots of economic crisis and poverty', saprin.org/global_rpt.htm. **29** P Sparr, *Mortgaging women's lives*, Zed Press, 1994. **30** Lori Pfingst, 'Women, work and Washington's economy', Washington State Budget and Policy Center, Feb 2012.

7 Redesigning the global economy

Globalization is increasing inequality and entrenching poverty worldwide as national governments lose the ability to control their development strategies and policies. Political solutions are needed to reinvigorate democratic control both North and South. But political reforms need to be combined with structural reforms. These should put meaningful employment and human rights at the heart of economic policy, boost local control and decision-making and restore the ecological health and natural capital of our planet.

Economic globalization is a powerful movement of people, goods, capital and ideas – driven by ideology, self-interest and bottom-line notions of economic efficiency.

But it is not a democratic process. For the most part it has proceeded without the approval or knowledge of those who have been most directly affected by the great economic upheavals of the past 35 years.

While it is true that globalization has boosted growth and lifted millions out of poverty, the process has been uneven. Cycles of boom and bust have produced growing inequality and widespread insecurity, tossing millions to the margins, North and South. It has also radically altered social relationships, stripping age-old cultures of their identity and threatening the environmental health of the planet.

Most of the measurable gains have been in Asia, especially in China and India. New investment, coupled with cheap labor and business-friendly governments, led to sustained growth in those two countries. That combination has reduced the number of extreme poor by half a billion since 1990, no small achievement.

In the past 30 years China has become the engine of

global manufacturing, flooding the world with mass-produced consumer goods. The Chinese economy has been booming. When the rest of the world slumped after the 2008 recession, China grew by 8.7 per cent in 2009. In the previous three decades the country's annual GDP growth averaged 10.2 per cent. China now uses nearly half the world's steel and cement. It's also the world's second-largest oil consumer after the US, and the world's biggest producer and consumer of coal. As a result of the country's astonishing success in reducing poverty, Chinese planners have begun deliberately to throttle back growth, aiming to stimulate the domestic economy at the expense of exports. This adjustment has spooked commodity-dependent countries around the globe that have ridden the coat tails of the Chinese boom. The US Conference Board expects the Chinese economy to ease to 5.5-per-cent growth by 2019. Despite this planned slowdown, its economy will soon outstrip the US. The investment bank Goldman Sachs predicts China will be the world's number one economic power by 2026. It's already the largest trading nation, with 2013 exports totalling $2.2 trillion. (The value of US exports for the same year was $1.57 trillion.)

But growth in both China and India has come with a huge cost: poisoned water, deadly air, depleted soils, the world's worst acid rain, and, in China, the largest migration from the countryside to urban areas in history.

According to the Worldwatch Institute: 'Land degradation, depleted aquifers, water pollution and urban claims on land and water are nibbling away at China and India's agricultural foundations – and may soon make it impossible for them to meet their rapidly expanding food needs.'[1]

Rapid growth has also heightened regional disparities and increased the gap between rich and poor. On average, workers in Indian cities earn nearly 40 per cent more than those in the countryside. In China, wage gaps are greatest between the booming east-coast cities and poorer rural areas. A Peking University study found that the average annual income for a Shanghai family in 2012 was $4,700 while the average in the northwest province of Gansu was under $2,000.[2] According to an Asian Development Bank study, China is now East Asia's second most unequal country after Nepal. The same Peking University survey found that the top five per cent of the country's households scooped up 23 per cent of total household income in 2012, while the bottom five per cent earned a mere 0.1 per cent. The poor are clearly better off but the rich are getting richer much faster. China still has 600 million citizens living on less than $2 a day and India has another 800 million in the same boat.

Fearing social unrest as inequality grows, former President Hu Jintao admitted that China needs to build a 'more balanced and harmonious society'. Signs of social discontent are multiplying. Strikes, walkouts and demonstrations are commonplace despite the Chinese state's willingness to crush dissent. China spends more on internal policing than it does on its military.

Typical was an April 2014 protest at the Taiwanese-owned Yue Yuen factory in Dongguan, 100 kilometers northwest of Hong Kong. The company is a major supplier of shoes for both Adidas and Nike. Thousands of employees at the 40,000-worker plant walked out in a dispute over social-security benefits and higher wages. 'Workers today are more aware of what they are entitled to in legal rights,' Geoffrey Crothall of the Hong Kong-based *China Labour Bulletin* told *Business Week* magazine.[3]

Meanwhile, globalization has all but completely ignored other parts of the world. In sub-Saharan Africa, between 1990 and 2002, per-capita income didn't rise at all. The number of people living on less than a dollar a day increased by a third, to more than 330 million. As UNDP notes, income inequality is increasing in countries that account for more than 80 per cent of the world's population.

Says Indian economist Jayati Ghosh: 'Despite popular perceptions, a net transfer of jobs from North to South did not take place... Instead, technological change meant fewer workers could generate more output. Old jobs in the South were lost or became precarious and the majority of new jobs were insecure and low paying.'[4]

This same pattern has been repeated across the so-called 'advanced' nations as companies cut staff, wages and benefits. Indeed, the 'race to the bottom' is one of the basic tropes of corporate globalization. A new study by former World Bank economist Branko Milanovic reinforces the notion of income inequality on a global scale. Milanovic shows that income gains in the decade prior to 2008 were divided between the super elites, the top tenth of one per cent, and what might be called the 'global middle' – essentially the rising Chinese and Indian middle class. For everyone else – mostly middle-class workers in the West – incomes have barely budged. The overwhelming majority of 'losers', says Milanovic, are from the 'old, conventional' rich world, 'predominantly the people who in their countries belong to the lower halves of national income distributions'. The concern, he says, is that 'the continued hollowing out of the middle class in the rich world, combined with growth of incomes at the top, could imply a movement away from democracy and toward forms of plutocracy'.[5]

Another world is possible

There is no doubt that what globalization purports to promise – increasing prosperity and decreasing poverty – is both compelling and necessary. And the forces behind this new global vision are formidable. But a top-down, unequal globalization is not inevitable. We can make the system work in a more just way. The economic structures that shape extraction, production and distribution are human-made. The institutions that make the rules governing the operation of the world economy are human-made. And the politicians that we elect to govern us are people too. Change is possible.

The crisis of globalization is a unique opportunity to address core issues of democracy and human development. It has invigorated a worldwide people's movement whose loud demands for change are attracting attention and support: from consumers, environmentalists, trade unionists, women's groups, religious activists, farmers, human rights advocates and ordinary citizens.

The World Social Forum has been one of the most visible expressions of opposition – an annual gathering of thousands of such groups from around the globe. The WSF was born in the aftermath of massive demonstrations against the World Trade Organization in Seattle in November 1999. It was initially organized to coincide with the annual gathering of political and business leaders at the World Economic Forum in Davos, Switzerland. The first three WSF meetings were held in Porto Alegre, Brazil. The fourth forum in Mumbai in 2004 drew more than 100,000 people. The 2013 meeting was in Tunis, the city that launched the 'Arab Spring' protest movement in January 2011. Activists from more than 150 countries have attended these yearly events but the WSF has also spawned dozens of local, regional and national social forums. These face-to-face encounters provide citizen groups with a chance to compare notes, to strategize and to hammer out alternatives to the prevailing model of economic globalization. This is not an 'anti' globalization movement as much as it is a 'pro' people's movement. The motto of the WSF is 'another world is possible'. It is, in essence, a network of networks focusing on global issues of social and economic justice, interacting when necessary, but mostly working independently on their own issues in their own countries or communities.

The Social Forum movement has so far managed to avoid fracturing into sectarianism and has avoided alliance with specific political parties – to its credit.

On the other hand, the network has been sharply criticized for relying on funding from corporate sources, including the Ford Foundation and other liberal granting organizations under the umbrella of the Engaged Donors for Global Equity (EDGE). But 'politics is the art of compromise' as the saying goes – the terrain is tricky. The WSF understands that, in order to influence change, the movement needs to remain independent of formal politics, acting instead as a conscience and a goad. And there is good reason for this. The powerful gatekeepers of the global economic system can force even the most progressive political leaders into tight corners. Yesterday's hero, bravely confronting the IMF or the WTO, can quickly collapse in the face of fierce pressures from international capital and become tomorrow's victim of corporate collusion.

Like the World Social Forum, the Occupy Wall Street (OWS) movement was a direct response to the failures of globalization, specifically the rising tide of economic inequality. The movement began quietly in September 2011 when several thousand people pitched tents in a small park in lower Manhattan. 'We are the 99%' was their slogan. It caught on, capturing in a short phrase the discontent and injustice of a broken global economy that was bypassing the vast majority. OWS triggered a wave of parallel protests in North America and across Europe, helping to shine the spotlight of public opinion on the long-festering but largely ignored issue of income inequality. Since then the issue has gone viral, seen by all but hidebound conservatives as a critical problem urgently needing attention. Critics, like UC Berkeley economics professor Emmanual Saez, have written that exploding wealth inequality is 'a direct threat to the cherished American ideals of meritocracy and opportunity'.[6] Saez found that 95 per cent of income gains in the US since 2009 have gone to the top one per cent. Meanwhile, Saez's colleague, French economist Thomas Piketty, saw his book, *Capital in the 21st*

Century, soar to the top of the bestseller lists. Piketty's detailed broadside against inequality quickly caught the attention of policymakers, reinforcing the message first raised by OWS and since backed by UN agencies like UNICEF, NGOs like Oxfam and millions of concerned citizens from Bogotá to Bangkok.

Other campaigns to rein in the globalization juggernaut have succeeded in educating millions about global inequalities. The Jubilee 2000 campaign to cancel Third World debt galvanized tens of thousands of supporters, both North and South. More recently, the Make Poverty History movement and the global Trade Justice Campaign have continued to push for significant changes to the world trading system to improve the lives of the world's poor. Even so, industrialized nations still drag their feet, refusing to lower subsidies and open the door to Southern exports. Commenting on his own country's predicament, Filipino Congress member Walden Bello noted: 'Three decades of export-oriented growth have resulted in trade accounting for some 30 per cent of gross domestic product. WTO-imposed liberalization has converted the country from a net food-exporting country into a net food-importing one... The main pillar of the economy is now the export of labor, with some 10 per cent of the country's 90 million people working and living outside the country.'[7]

Political leaders are feeling increased pressure to improve the lot of those who have been bypassed by progress. Across Latin America, opposition to globalization has exploded since Brazil's 1998 economic crisis and the collapse of the Argentinean economy in 2002 – both of which were triggered by hard-line IMF policies and meddling by financial speculators. Following the 2002 election of former labor activist Ignacio 'Lula' da Silva in Brazil, leaders opposed to wide-open markets were elected in Argentina, Ecuador, Venezuela, Bolivia, Nicaragua, El Salvador, Uruguay and Chile. At the November 2005 Summit of the Americas in Buenos

Aires, many of those nations spearheaded opposition to the proposed Free Trade Area of the Americas (FTAA), derailing plans to extend free trade from the Arctic to Patagonia. The dissenting nations claimed in the Summit's closing declaration that 'conditions do not exist to attain a hemispheric free-trade accord that is balanced and fair with access to markets and free of subsidies and distorted commercial practices.' By 2015 there were few national governments in Latin America willing to give free rein to open markets.

Even so, national differences continue to shape policy. In recent years countries like Argentina, Venezuela and Brazil have been wary of another free trade proposal, the Trans-Pacific Partnership, while nations like Chile, Peru and Mexico, encouraged by their own business leaders, have been more open to the idea.

Those who control the global economy understand that popular opposition to the project of economic globalization is growing. More than a decade ago, at the 1999 Asia Pacific Economic Co-operation (APEC) meetings in New Zealand, then-US trade negotiator Charlene Barshefsky admitted that the single greatest threat to globalization is 'the absence of public support'. Her concerns are justified. There is now a worldwide citizens' movement attempting to rethink the global economy from the ground up. It is a movement which is spreading and becoming stronger by the day. And it is premised on one shared, central truth. The only way to convince states to act in the interests of their citizens is to construct a system that will put people at the center of economic activity. And critically, the economic rights of individuals and communities must be in harmony with environmental limits.

Inevitably, this is a question of politics as much as economics. What's encouraging is that millions of people in scores of countries around the globe are actively lobbying, debating and campaigning for change.

What follows are a few of the ideas currently being discussed.

Abolish the Bretton Woods institutions

The IMF, along with sister organizations the World Bank and the World Trade Organization, should be abolished – replaced with completely new organizations with new mandates and new staff.

The new agencies should be decentralized, regional institutions built on co-operative principles rather than free trade and capital mobility. They must become more democratic and more focused on the needs and interests of the citizens of the world rather than fixated on narrow market goals.

This regional approach is now being seriously considered.

The continuing global financial crisis has prompted even mainstream political leaders to speculate about a new European equivalent of the IMF. When Greece's debt soared in early 2010, the country teetered on the brink of bankruptcy. The European Union's concern was the impact of the plunging euro on the rest of the EU. The possible solution: a European equivalent of the IMF – a European Monetary Fund – to provide financial backing for Greece. 'We want to be able to resolve our problems in the future without the IMF,' said German Chancellor Angela Merkel.

These new institutions will need to be more accountable to all their members – with more democratic and more transparent decision-making.

In the past the Fund has been arrogant and closed to criticism. New regionally based agencies would need to move beyond finance ministry officials to talk (and listen) to trade unions, peasant organizations, women's groups and non-governmental organizations – the people who will be on the receiving end of the social impact of any agreement. To improve accountability, there should be regular external evaluations of whatever programs and policies are put in place.

Critically, structural-adjustment policies – political, social and economic conditions attached to balance-of-payment loans – should be jettisoned. The standard recipe – austerity, balanced budgets and 'efficient markets' – should not be allowed to erode national sovereignty, or interfere with the decisions of elected governments. Coercion is by nature anti-democratic.

The central goal of these new regional organizations must be to improve the lives of ordinary people – to alleviate poverty, to wipe out Southern debt, to promote equity and to encourage efficient, green technologies. Markets should serve people, not the other way round.

As long as a global market economy exists – and it doesn't show signs of disappearing soon – multilateral institutions will be necessary to regulate and manage the flow of capital, goods and services. But, in the words of Keynes, we should 'minimize' rather than 'maximize economic entanglement among nations.'

Co-operation must be the watchword of any new regional institutions. A single-minded, inflexible approach based on market fundamentalism will exacerbate the instability and inequality of the global market. By scrapping the Bretton Woods trio – the IMF, the World Bank and the WTO – we can start afresh to build new institutions with a moral purpose and a democratic mandate which will work to the benefit of the majority of the world's citizens.

Support a tax on financial speculation

Unregulated investment has turned the global economy into a casino where speculators search for instant profits, ignoring the human consequences of their actions. Nowhere was this more evident than in the world-shaking financial crisis which erupted in 2008. The combination of sub-prime mortgages, speculation and greed by banks, insurance companies and investment firms triggered the most severe economic downturn since the Great Depression. By March 2009 more than $50 trillion of assets were wiped out, including $7 trillion in US stock-market wealth and $6 trillion in US housing wealth.[8]

Currency markets can be useful – taking the worry out of international buying and selling by figuring out today what a future purchase will cost. But it's estimated that just 2-4 per cent of currency trading has to do with real market exchanges. The rest is pure speculation, making money off money. A tax on speculative dealings in foreign currencies, shares and other securities would put people ahead of profits.

In 1978, the Nobel Prize-winning economist James Tobin proposed that a small worldwide tariff (less than half of one per cent) be levied by all major countries on foreign-exchange transactions in order to 'throw some sand in the wheels' of speculative flows. The tax would have no effect on serious long-term investors. A tax of .05 per cent would dampen speculation while stabilizing global markets and capturing much-needed funds for global development. According to UNCTAD, daily foreign-exchange trading now tops $4 trillion, while only one per cent of foreign exchange trading is actually related to merchandise trade. Even if the trade fell by 25 per cent after a transaction tax was imposed, it would still yield billions in revenues for the public purse.

There is a significant movement to back such a tax. France and Germany have signalled support and in early 2010 more than 350 economists urged the G20 governments to adopt the so-called 'Robin Hood' tax as 'a matter of urgency'. The tax has won widespread support from charities, environmental groups, trade unions, celebrities, financiers, religious leaders and even a few politicians. Columbia University economist Jeffrey Sachs says: 'The transaction tax is technically feasible and morally essential to repair the mess made by the banks.' The goal is to dampen speculation and to raise funds to support global development – a rare opportunity to capture the enormous wealth of an untaxed sector and redirect it towards the public good.

At this point the main barrier is not technical, it's political. The tax is seen as a threat by the financial community and has met with stiff resistance by a sector with massive political clout. The very idea of putting people ahead of markets challenges the foundations of the current global economic model and those who control it.

Control capital for the public good

The world was a heartbeat away from complete economic collapse in 2008. Only a multi-billion-dollar bailout by national governments helped stave off disaster. Globalization – the freewheeling era of unregulated capital flows and free markets – brought us to the brink. And we will bear the social and psychological scars for years to come. The costs of the crisis have been huge: industries have been shuttered while trade has plummeted and unemployment has spiked. Social services have been slashed in the wake of government budget cuts while cynical politicians stir up anti-immigrant bigotry. Renewed recession is still a looming threat.

In countries like Iceland and Ireland the bailouts of the banks cost more than two-and-a-half times the national income. And governments everywhere are faced with massive deficits which may haunt them for decades. Memories are short: the deficit hawks warn that we will all have to tighten our belts to pay for the malfeasance of the financial community. But we must not forget what caused the crisis in the first place: a globalized financial system which was unaccountable, unregulated and driven by greed. Now is the time for a clean start. We have the greatest opportunity since the Great Depression of the 1930s to restructure global economic relations in a more democratic and sustainable way.

Here are some brief notes on alternative strategies to economic globalization that could take us in a new direction.

Regulate the financial system

Capital needs to be used as an instrument of development, not as a tool for turning a quick profit at the expense of people and the Earth. Democratic control of capital means strict regulation of banks and investment firms. They should not be in the business of gambling.

Close tax havens

They serve no useful purpose except to help corporations hide their profits and to make rich individuals even richer. They should be closed immediately and international rules should be put in place to allow tax officials in all countries to exchange financial information and to end banking secrecy.

Break up the big banks

If they're too big to fail, they're too big. Period. After the meltdown of 2008, governments in Britain, the US and elsewhere became part-owners of some of the biggest banks and insurance companies. But the crash also spawned even larger banks as 'winners' swallowed 'losers'. The big banks should be broken into smaller units so that if they do fail they don't threaten the entire system. At the moment their gambling is risk-free; if they lose, taxpayers pick up the tab.

Fix foreign investment

Foreign investment should be welcome only if social obligations are met; governments should be able to restrict the repatriation of profits. Governments should also have the right to require corporations, both foreign and domestic, to meet basic social obligations and development priorities such as labor standards, job quotas, environmental safeguards and social-security contributions. Free trade should not override the democratic will of the electorate.

Promote public enterprise

Governments have a responsibility to use tax revenues for protecting the 'commons' through public investments. These could include: exercising public ownership over key sectors of the economy; establishing social programs and public services; safeguarding ecologically sensitive areas; and protecting cultural heritage.

People before profits

A foreign corporation should not be able to demand compensation for an environmental law that placed a quota on the export of a nonrenewable resource or a health ban on the sale of toxic substances. Nor should a foreign company claim compensation for loss of future profits because government actions prevent a planned investment from going ahead.

Go local

The export-oriented model needs to be jettisoned and free trade corralled. The United States cannot continue as 'consumer of last resort' for global exports. Countries need to redirect production towards domestic needs. Trade policy, including tariffs and quotas, should be used to protect the local economy and to boost domestic manufacturing. This will both strengthen community bonds and benefit the environment.

Support fair trade

'Max Havelaar', the first fair-trade initiative, was launched in Holland in 1988. The name was taken from a fictional character who had opposed the exploitation of coffee pickers in Dutch colonies. In 1997, the Fairtrade Labelling Organizations International (FLO) brought Max Havelaar together with counterparts in other countries. Now known as Fairtrade International, the organization includes three producer networks, an independent certification body and 25 fair-trade organizations in Europe, Japan, North America, Mexico, Australia and New Zealand/Aotearoa. Meanwhile the World Fair Trade Organization gathers together organizations all over the world that demonstrate 100-per-cent commitment to fair trade in all their business activities and subscribe to a set of key principles. It's a stunning achievement that producer networks in Africa, Latin America and Asia now represent nearly two million farmers in more than 70 countries.

Compared with conventional trading structures, these Alternative Trade Organizations offer higher returns to producers in the developing world through direct trade and fair prices. The fair-trade movement is a response to a global trading system that is both unjust and exploitative – global trading rules are rigged to benefit the rich and marginalize the poor. Fixing the global system will take major institutional changes and a determined campaign.

Unregulated trade allows corporations to pit workers against each another, to reduce the bargaining strength of trade unions, to strip away benefits, to ignore dangerous working conditions and to reduce wages.

Instead, trade agreements must bolster the rights of working people by promoting labor rights – including the freedom to form trade unions and bargain collectively. Free trade is a social issue as well as an economic one. To attract investors, countries compete to lower costs. That can trigger a 'race to the bottom' where job-hungry nations offer cheap labor, weak environmental laws, lax health-and-safety standards or reduced social services. Governments must have the right to regulate foreign investment to protect their citizens and to link investment to national development priorities.

Nations should have the power to establish and defend intellectual property rules that protect the interests of their citizens. Trade agreements must guarantee access to essential drugs, prohibit the erosion of traditional cultures and protect indigenous knowledge and biodiversity.

If democracy is to have meaning, citizens must help to formulate global trade rules. These agreements must promote civil and political rights as well as the social, cultural, economic and environmental rights of peoples and communities.

In the meantime, the fair-trade movement provides a

chance to learn about the blatant unfairness of the global trading system. And to set standards that could redefine global trade to include social and environmental considerations.

1 *State of the World 2006*, Worldwatch Institute, WW Norton, New York, 2006. **2** Edward Wong, 'Survey in China Shows a Wide Gap in Income', *New York Times*, 19 Jul 2013. **3** Dexter Roberts, 'Workers Continue to Strike at Nike and Adidas Supplier in Southern China', businessweek.com, 17 Apr 2014. **4** 'Downside up', *New Internationalist*, No 430, Mar 2010. **5** Branko Milanovic, 'Winners of globalization: The rich and the Chinese middle class. Losers: the American middle class', *The World Post*, 21 Jan 2014. **6** Michael Hiltzik, 'US income inequality is bad, but wealth inequality is a bigger problem', *Los Angeles Times*, 24 Oct 2014. **7** Walden Bello, 'Reflections of a Filipino MP', *New Internationalist*, No 430, Mar 2010. **8** John Bellamy Foster, 'The Age of Monopoly-Finance Capital', *Monthly Review,* Vol 61, No 9, Feb 2010.

Index Page numbers in **bold** refer to main subjects of boxed text.